THE EVERYTHING KIDS'

Hanukkah Puzzle and Activity Book

Games, crafts, trivia, songs, and traditions
to celebrate the festival of lights

Beth L. Blair and Jennifer A. Ericsson
with Rabbi Hyim Shafner

A adamsmedia
Avon, Massachusetts

PUBLISHER Karen Cooper

DIRECTOR OF ACQUISITIONS AND INNOVATION Paula Munier

MANAGING EDITOR, EVERYTHING SERIES Lisa Laing

COPY CHIEF Casey Ebert

ACQUISITIONS EDITORS Kerry Smith and Katie McDonough

DEVELOPMENT EDITOR Elizabeth Kassab

EDITORIAL ASSISTANT Hillary Thompson

Published by Adams Media, an F+W Publications Company
57 Littlefield Street, Avon, MA 02322. U.S.A.
www.adamsmedia.com

ISBN-10: 1-59869-788-9
ISBN-13: 978-1-59869-788-9

Printed in the United States of America.

J I H G F E D C B A

This publication is designed to provide accurate and authoritative information with regard to
the subject matter covered. It is sold with the understanding that the publisher is not engaged
in rendering legal, accounting, or other professional advice. If legal advice or other expert
assistance is required, the services of a competent professional person should be sought.
　　　　　—From a *Declaration of Principles* jointly adopted by a Committee of the
American Bar Association and a Committee of Publishers and Associations

Many of the designations used by manufacturers and sellers to distinguish their products are
claimed as trademarks. When those designations appear in this book and Adams Media was
aware of a trademark claim, the designations have been printed with initial capital letters.

Cover illustrations by Dana Regan.
Interior illustrations by Kurt Dolber.
Puzzles by Beth L. Blair.

This book is available at quantity discounts for bulk purchases.
For information, please call 1-800-289-0963.

Visit the entire Everything® series at *www.everything.com*

Contents

ACKNOWLEDGMENTS

Our deepest thanks goes to Rabbi Hyim Shafner, our consultant on this project. He graciously and quickly answered all of our many questions.

Shalom (peace),
Jennifer A. Ericsson
Beth L. Blair

Introduction

Happy Hanukkah!

In November or December each year, Jewish people around the world celebrate the eight days of Hanukkah. It commemorates the fight for religious freedom by the Maccabees against the Syrians more than 2,000 years ago. It also celebrates the miracle of the oil, which burned for eight days in the Holy Temple. The amazing thing is that everyone believed there was only enough oil to burn for one day!

The eight days of Hanukkah can be full of family, friends, food, and fun. You might be lighting the hanukkiah, spinning the dreidel, feasting on latkes, or singing "Maoz Tzur." But somewhere among the festivities, you might like some quiet time alone to try your hand at a Hanukkah puzzle or two.

Included in *The Everything® Kids' Hanukkah Puzzle and Activity Book* are more than 100 different mazes, word searches, acrostics, rebuses, codes, and other types of puzzles. You'll also find games, activities, and crafts that are lots of fun to share with siblings, friends, cousins, aunts and uncles, and even grandmas and grandpas!

Do you have to be Jewish to enjoy this book? Absolutely not! Anyone interested in learning about this beautiful and holy celebration should grab a pen or pencil and start puzzling. We've included a sample puzzle to get you started.

Turn Around

The story of Hanukkah reminds us how the Jewish people changed a bad situation into a positive one!

Search for the <u>opposite</u> of these words.

DARK **WAR**
EMPTY **COLD**
HATE **WEAK**
DIRTY **UGLY**

```
B E C B E A U
B A L I G H T
E S E C N C E
A N A L G L C
U R N F I E A
T S F C U A E
I P T L O L P
F E C R E A L
U S T U O E B
L O V E T N E
A W A R M U G
```

Chapter 1

The Story of Hanukkah

Hanukkah Beginnings

Hanukkah is a Jewish religious holiday. Its origins go back more than 2,000 years to the land of Judea. But if you search a modern atlas for Judea, you won't find it! Break the code and fill the correct letters into the boxes.

one before J	between R and T	two after P	first one	four before I	between K and M
I	S	R	A	E	L

When you are finished, you will know what Judea is called today.

Extra Fun:
Fill in all the blocks with a horizontal line. You will discover this country's official language.

–	/	–	/	–	–	\	–	–	|	/	–	–	–	/	–	–	\	–	/	|	\	–
–	\	–	/	–	|	/	–	/	–	\	–	/	–	|	–	\	|	–	\	|	|	–
–	–	–	|	–	–	/	–	–	|	\	–	–	\	/	–	–	–	/	–	\	–	\
–	/	–	\	–	/	–	\	–	–	/	\	–	/	|	–	–	/	–	–	/	–	–
–	|	–	/	–	|	–	–	|	/	–	|	–	|	–	–	\	\	–	\	–	/	

Holy City, Holy Temple

The most important building in the Jewish religion is the temple, where Jews go to worship. It contains all the important religious items for their faith, including the Torah scrolls, Ark, and Eternal Light. In the land of Judea, the Holy Temple was built on the top of a mountain!

To learn the name of the city where the Holy Temple was located, start at the letter marked with a dot. Move clockwise, and collect every other letter. Write them, in order, in the boxes.

The Holy Temple

Many Versus One

In 175 B.C.E., King Antiochus ruled the land of Judea. He was Greek and wanted to make his whole kingdom follow the same religion he did! Part of Antiochus's plan was to invade Jerusalem and take over the Holy Temple. Inside the temple he placed statues of the different Greek gods he worshiped. To the Jews, this was a BIG problem. Why?

Unscramble each word in this sentence to find out.

HTE EWJS

LIBEEVE NI

LYNO NOE

OGD.

What Is B.C.E.?

Are you confused by the letters you see after a date from long, long ago? Using a simple number substitution (1=A, 2=B, 3=C, and so on), you can see for yourself what those letters stand for.

Okay, so what does this mean? Break the Looking Glass code to find out!

2 - 5 - 6 - 15 - 18 - 5

3 - 15 - 13 - 13 - 15 - 14

5 - 18 - 1

The Common Era began at year 1. That means if you are in the year 2010, the Common Era began 2010 years ago! Dates that have a B.C.E. after them are even longer ago than that — these dates are <u>before</u> the Common Era started!

Brave Decision

In 167 B.C.E., soldiers arrived at the village of Modin to make Mattathias, a respected Jewish priest, bow down to a Greek god. He refused. When another villager tried to do it, Mattathias killed him, and a soldier too! Then he fled to the hills with his sons. What did Mattathias say to the villagers as he left Modin?

To find out, write the letters from the scattered pieces into the proper spaces in the grid.

Helpful Hint:
Match the pattern of the black boxes.

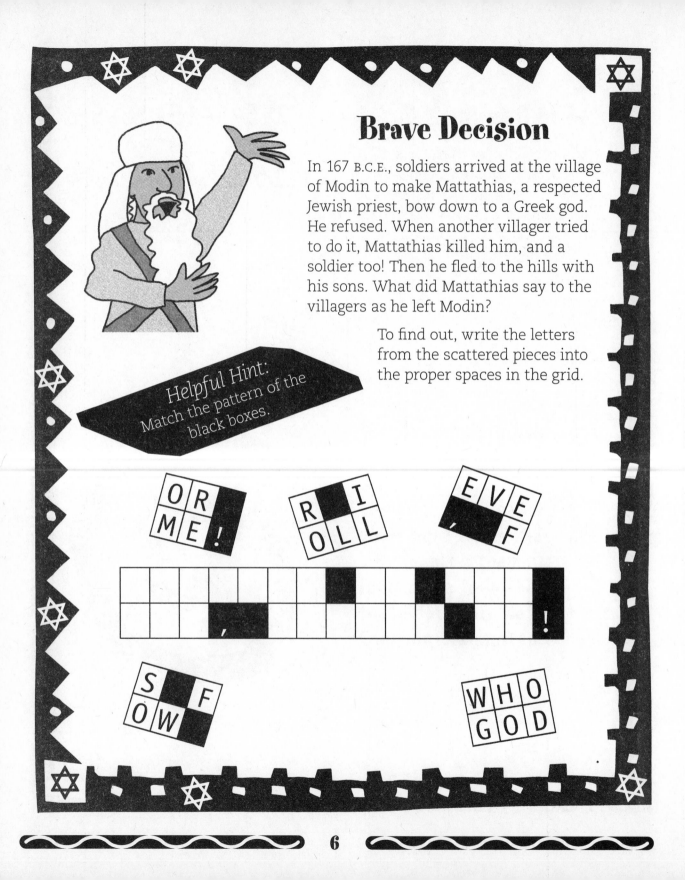

Rebellion!

Mattathias and his followers hid in caves in the hills. They were greatly outnumbered by the king's soldiers, but they did not give up!

Hidden in the grid are five words that mean "to fight." Take one letter from each column, moving from left to right. Each letter can only be used once! One word has been done for you.

B O S I A T
C E T T L K
A T T A C T
R A M B L E
R E V O S T

1. _B A T T L E_
2. _____
3. _____
4. _____
5. _____

Which Son?

Mattathias had five sons. When he died, one of them took over as leader. Use the following clues to determine which son it was.

Clue 1
He wore a light-colored robe.

Clue 2
His name did not have a "Z".

Clue 3
He had curly hair.

Clue 4
He did not wear sandals.

JONATHAN APPHUS   ELEAZAR AVARON   JUDAH MACCABEUS   SIMON THASSI   JOHANAN GADDI

Why Fight?

The Jews who fought with Judah Maccabeus were known as the Maccabees. They hid in the hills and had few weapons. King Antiochus's army had a lot more men and better weapons than the Maccabees. Why did Judah and his people keep fighting the king when it seemed they could not win? Solve this puzzle to learn why!

Each of the clues suggests a word. Write the words on the lines, and then put each letter into the numbered grid. Work back and forth between the clues and the grid.

A. Opposite of day

__ __ __ __ __
31 35 36 5 14

B. Frozen water

__ __ __
27 22 33

C. Not rich

__ __ __ __
16 2 15 8

D. Part of your foot

__ __ __
24 29 10

E. Solid

__ __ __ __
7 21 32 13

F. Follows two

__ __ __ __ __
20 25 17 9 23

G. Lion's noise

__ __ __ __
28 12 18 3

H. Opposite of dry

__ __ __
30 6 4

I. Not hot

__ __ __ __
19 38 34 11

J. Overdue book penalty

__ __ __ __
1 37 39 26

Why did the Maccabees keep fighting against the king?

		1J	2C	3G		4H	5A	6H		
		7E	8C	9F	10D	11 I	12G	13E		
14A	15C		16C	17F	18G	19 I	20F	21E	22B	23F
	24D	25F	26J	27B	28G		29D	30H	31A	
	32E	33B	34I	35A	36A	37J	38I	39J		

Big in Battle

King Antiochus's army had many weapons to use in the fight against the Maccabees. They had swords, bows and arrows, and horses to ride. They had one other powerful weapon that was very big! Connect the dots from 1-53, and break the Vowel Switch code to see what it was!

ORMERUD ULUPHONTS

Tough Guys

The Maccabees would often sneak up on the king's army and launch a surprise attack. In Hebrew, the word "maccabee" describes something that hits hard and fast, just like the Maccabees! Fill in all the shapes with the letters H-A-R-D to find out what it is.

The Maccabees would strike like a...

Cleaning House

After three long years, the Maccabees finally defeated the king's army and reclaimed the Holy Temple! They cleaned it, removed the Greek statues, and made the temple ready to once again be a house of prayer for the Jewish people. Complete this puzzle to learn the name of the special ceremony held to make the temple holy again.

...AND STAY OUT!

1. Second ½ of PURE
2. Middle ⅓ of REDEEM
3. Third ¼ of BUILDING
4. First ½ of CALM
5. Last ⅔ of ACTION

Figure out which letters are described by each fraction. Print the letters in order, from left to right, in the boxes.

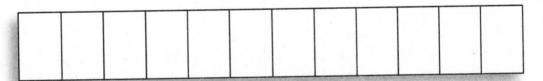

Replace the symbols with the correct vowels to learn a fun Hanukkah fact!

Th✳ w◆rd H⌖n⊗kk⌖h m✳⌖ns "d✳d◆c⌖t✳✦n" ✦n H✳br✳w.

Lighting the Lamp

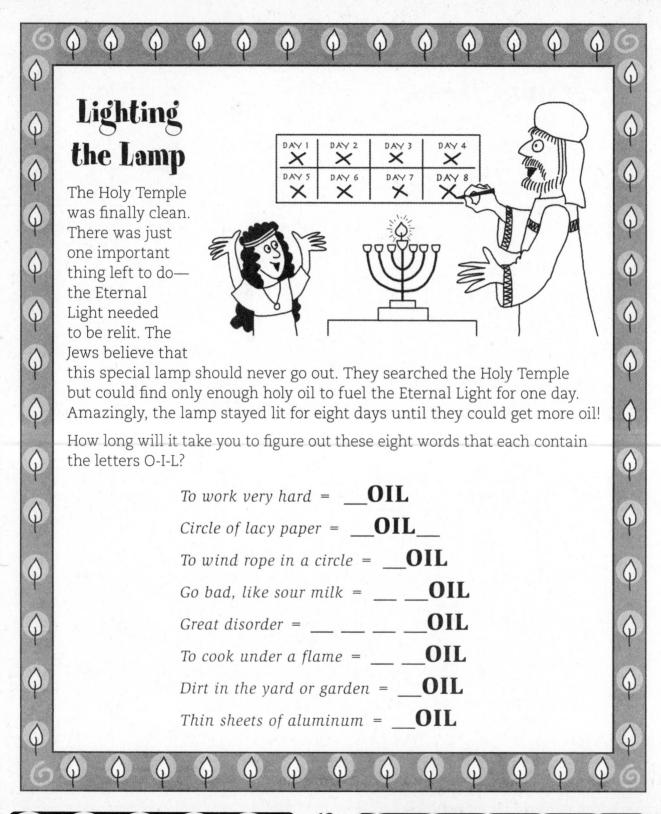

The Holy Temple was finally clean. There was just one important thing left to do—the Eternal Light needed to be relit. The Jews believe that this special lamp should never go out. They searched the Holy Temple but could find only enough holy oil to fuel the Eternal Light for one day. Amazingly, the lamp stayed lit for eight days until they could get more oil!

How long will it take you to figure out these eight words that each contain the letters O-I-L?

To work very hard = __**OIL**

Circle of lacy paper = __**OIL**__

To wind rope in a circle = __**OIL**

Go bad, like sour milk = __ __**OIL**

Great disorder = __ __ __ __**OIL**

To cook under a flame = __ __**OIL**

Dirt in the yard or garden = __**OIL**

Thin sheets of aluminum = __**OIL**

Amazing Events

When good things happen unexpectedly, it is definitely a cause for celebration! The Jews decided to commemorate two amazing events together by observing the eight days of Hanukkah.

1. Against all odds, Judah and the Maccabees defeated King Antiochus and reclaiMed the temple In JeRusalem.

* * * * * * *

2. The oil thAt should only have lasted one night, CuriousLy, burned for Eight dayS!

Read the sentences again and find the capital letters that do not belong. Place them in the boxes from left to right. You will learn what is at the very heart of the Hanukkah celebration!

Wonderful things that cannot be explained are called...

Light Up the Night

Hanukkah is celebrated for eight nights in memory of the eight nights that one small jar of oil burned in the Holy Temple. Because a candle is lit for each night of the holiday, Hanukkah is sometimes called by another name! To find out what it is, match the symbol on each candle to a letter. Write the letter in the flame.

A	E	F	G	H	I	L	O	S	T	V
☆	◉	◆	✦	✳	✡	✺	✩	✿	✶	❖

Cover Up

Before the Hanukkah rituals begin, all the men and boys in the family should cover their heads with a kippah. These are small caps that Jewish males wear while praying. To learn the reason for wearing a kippah, start at the letter marked with a dot. Pick up every other letter as you move counterclockwise around the rim.

Fun Fact: People who speak Yiddish would call this special cap a yarmulke.

_ _ _ _ _ _ _ _ _ _ _ _ _ _ _

Day Is Done

Like all Jewish holy days, Hanukkah begins at sundown. As the day draws to a close, families gather together in their homes to start the celebration. Make a path, creating compound words as you go, from SUNDOWN to HOUSEHOLD. You can move up and down and side to side, but not diagonally.

START

SUN	DAY	BREAK	FAST	RAN
DOWN	RIGHT	LEFT	TOWN	SOME
POUR	HAND	MADE	ME	COME
HOLD	BAG	UP	GRADE	BACK
ON	LADY	SHIP	SCHOOL	YARD
TIME	BUG	LAMP	HOUSE	HOLD

END

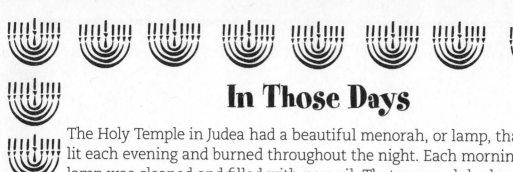

In Those Days

The Holy Temple in Judea had a beautiful menorah, or lamp, that was lit each evening and burned throughout the night. Each morning the lamp was cleaned and filled with new oil. That menorah had seven branches.

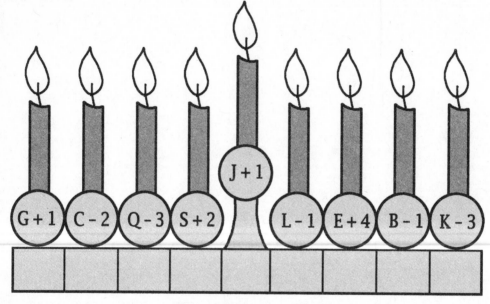

In This Time

Today during Hanukkah, a slightly different menorah is lit. It has nine branches, not seven. Eight of the branches symbolize the miracle that one day's worth of oil for the temple menorah burned for eight days. The ninth branch holds a candle that serves to light all the others!

The lamp used during Hanukkah has a special name in Hebrew. To learn what it is, solve the letter equations along the base of this menorah. Write the letters in the empty squares, then read the answer from left to right.

Three Blessings

Blessings are said each night of Hanukkah as the candles are being lit. On the first night of Hanukkah, all three blessings are said. For the next seven nights, only the first two blessings are recited.

We have given you four codes to choose from. The three blessings are found on the facing page. You must figure out which code is used for each blessing!

FIRST-TO-LAST CODE
The first letter of each word has been moved to the end of that word.

LAST-TO-FIRST CODE
The last letter of each word has been moved to the start of that word.

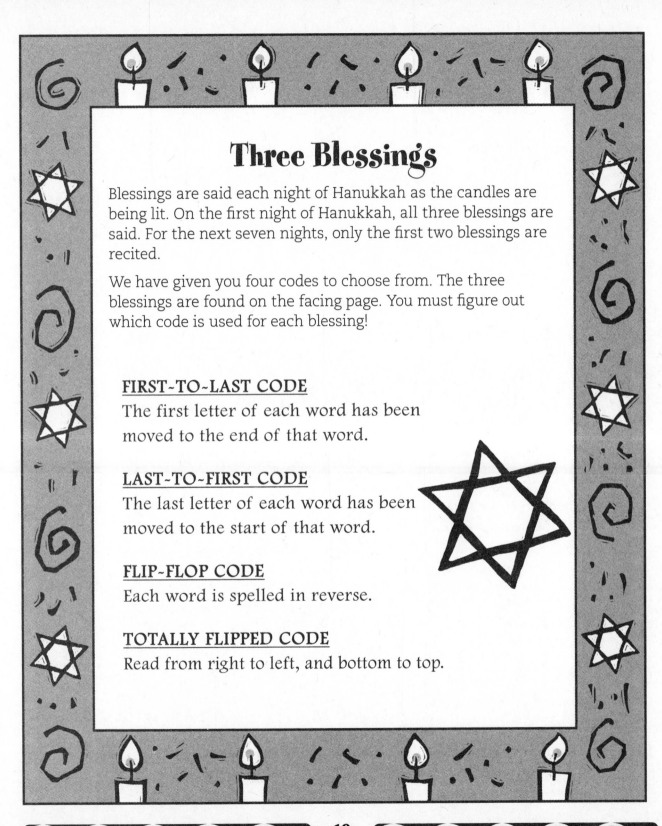

FLIP-FLOP CODE
Each word is spelled in reverse.

TOTALLY FLIPPED CODE
Read from right to left, and bottom to top.

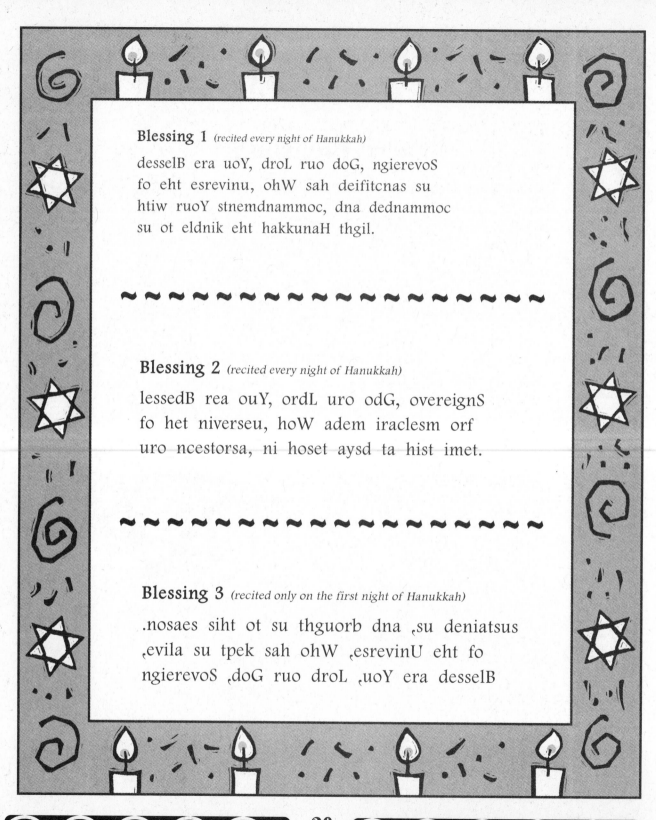

Blessing 1 *(recited every night of Hanukkah)*

desselB era uoY, droL ruo doG, ngierevoS
fo eht esrevinu, ohW sah deifitcnas su
htiw ruoY stnemdnammoc, dna dednammoc
su ot eldnik eht hakkunaH thgil.

~~~~~~~~~~~~~~~~~~~~~~~~~~~~~~~

Blessing 2 *(recited every night of Hanukkah)*

lessedB rea ouY, ordL uro odG, overeignS
fo het niverseu, hoW adem iraclesm orf
uro ncestorsa, ni hoset aysd ta hist imet.

~~~~~~~~~~~~~~~~~~~~~~~~~~~~~~~

Blessing 3 *(recited only on the first night of Hanukkah)*

.nosaes siht ot su thguorb dna ,su deniatsus
,evila su tpek sah ohW ,esrevinU eht fo
ngierevoS ,doG ruo droL ,uoY era desselB

Shining Servant

The eight side branches of a hanukkiah (Hanukkah menorah) are all the same height, but the ninth branch in the center is higher. It holds the special shammas, or servant candle. The shammas is the first candle lit each night. Then it is used to light all the other candles!

Shammas is a double-m word. Will you need help to fill in these other double-m words?

A wrapped Egyptian = _ _ M M _

Moving through water = _ _ _ M M _ _ _

Curved punctuation mark = _ _ M M _

Living forever = _ M M _ _ _ _ _

To shine with faint light = _ _ _ M M _ _

A kid's word for stomach = _ _ M M _

---

represent
3

anything
12

not
8

else
13

miracle
5

for
11

They
6

be
9

Hanukkah
1

a
4

used
10

should
7

candles
2

Why Use a Shammas?

Put the numbered words in the correct spaces to find out!

___ ___ ___   ___ ___   ___ ___ ___   ___ ___   ___ .
     1   2   3   4   5

___ ___   ___ ___ ___ ___ ___ ___ ___ !
 6   7   8   9   10   11   12   13

Marvelous Matchbox

During the Hanukkah celebration, your family will be using a lot of matches to light the candles in their menorahs. This holiday deserves a special box of matches!

What you need:
tacky glue
1 large box of wooden kitchen matches
1 piece of white felt, cut 4½ x 8 inches
blue glitter glue
short emery board

Alternative: Use blue felt and silver glitter glue.

What you do:

1. Squeeze tacky glue on one of the wide sides of the matchbox.

2. Turn the box over and carefully place it in the middle of the piece of felt. The same amount of felt should show on both sides of the box.

3. Press gently to help the glue stick to the felt.

4. Wrap the felt around the box of matches. The ends of the felt should overlap a little bit.

5. Lift the top piece of felt. Squeeze a line of tacky glue along the edge of the felt underneath.

6. Gently press the top layer of felt onto the glue.

7. Check that the drawer of the matchbox still opens. The wrapper should be snug, but not enough to keep the drawer from opening.

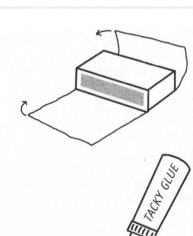

Fun Fact: For almost 1,000 years, the Star of David has been a symbol of the Jewish religion.

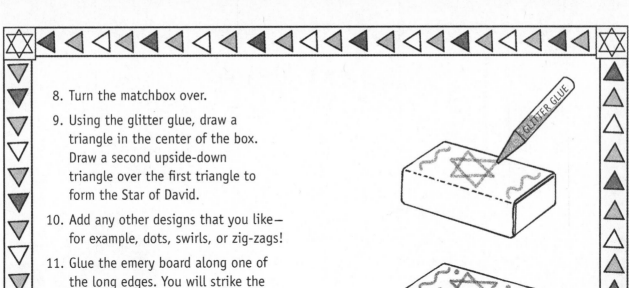

8. Turn the matchbox over.

9. Using the glitter glue, draw a triangle in the center of the box. Draw a second upside-down triangle over the first triangle to form the Star of David.

10. Add any other designs that you like— for example, dots, swirls, or zig-zags!

11. Glue the emery board along one of the long edges. You will strike the matches on this.

12. Let the matchbox dry thoroughly.

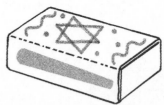

Hanukkah? Chanukah?

The Hebrew language has sounds that don't occur in English. For instance, the "H" sound starts farther back in the throat, sounding a bit like the English "K." That's why different people spell Hanukkah differently. They are using English letters to try to create the sound of Hebrew!

Try to say these Hanukkah tongue twisters quickly, three times each!

✡ **A HUNDRED HANUKKAH HICCUPS**

✡ **CHUNKY CHANUKAH CHIPS**

✡ **HAPPY HANUKKAH, HONEY!**

Proper Lighting

On the first night of Hanukkah, one candle is placed in the menorah all the way to the right. Then the shammas is lit, and it is used to light that candle. Each night after that, another candle is added. On the last night of Hanukkah there are nine candles burning brightly! Here's the tricky part—the candles are placed in the hanukkiah from right to left, but they are lit from left to right!

Use a blue marker to draw the candles for each night of Hanukkah. Use a yellow marker to draw the flames. Be sure to add the candles and light them in the correct order!

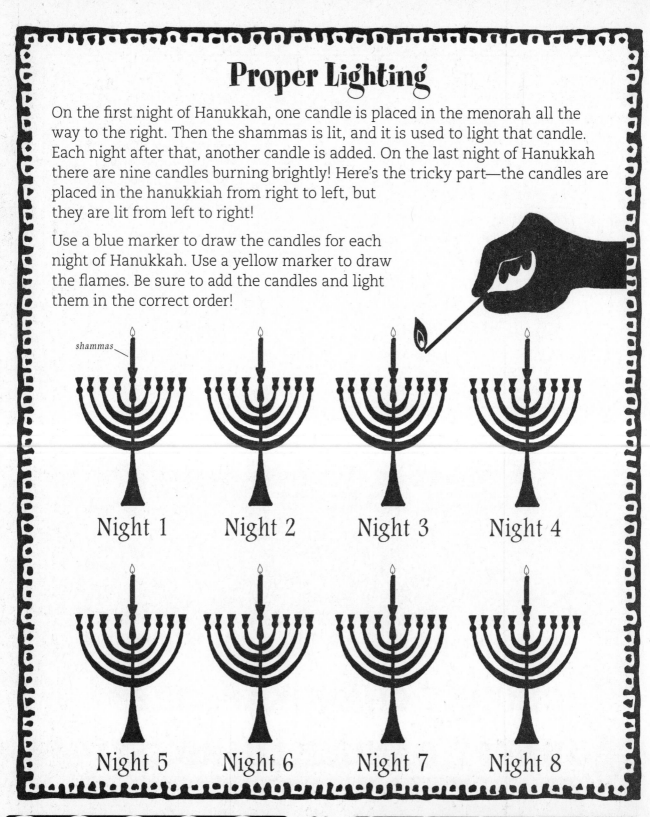

shammas

Night 1   Night 2   Night 3   Night 4

Night 5   Night 6   Night 7   Night 8

Show Off

Tradition calls for the lighted menorah to never be hidden. Connect the dots to learn where it should be displayed.

Can you break the Letter After code?

HM SGD

VHMCNV

Time to Share

In order to share the miracle of Hanukkah, the candles must stay lit for a minimum amount of time. Use the clues to figure out which times to cross off the list. The last time remaining is correct!

The candles...

...burn more than a quarter hour.

...do not burn for a whole day.

...burn less than 60 minutes.

5 *minutes*
15 *minutes*
30 *minutes*
1 *hour*
12 *hours*
24 *hours*

Eight in a Row

In the menorah, the eight candles representing the different nights of Hanukkah are placed at the same height. Drop the scrambled letters from each column into the spaces directly underneath. When you have correctly filled in the grid, you will know why this is so!

D	S			F			O		K	K	A	A		
I	A	Y	M	O	S	E		A	O	P	H	I	N	H
B	H	A	A	O	T	E	E	I	N	T	O	S	E	R
T	E	C	N	U	R	H	H	N	M	U	S	R	T	G
B					E			O				G		
		Y								K				
	S													
				T					H					

Counting Candles

How many candles does it take to light one hanukkiah for the eight nights of Hanukkah? Use the Candle Clues to figure out how many are used each night. Then add them all up!

First Night = ____

Second Night = ____

Third Night = ____

Fourth Night = ____

Fifth Night = ____

Sixth Night = ____

Seventh Night = ____

Eighth Night = ____

TOTAL =

Candle Clues

Each night a new shammas is used.

Each night an additional candle is lit.

Each night all new candles are used.

"Hyim! Enough already!"

"OK, Dad!"

Extra Fun:
Mr. and Mrs. Shafner and their two children each like to light their own hanukkiah! How many candles does their family use during the entire Hanukkah celebration?

Monika's Menorah

Can you find the one menorah
that matches Monika's list?

The menorah to look for has...
...room for 8 candles
(plus the shamas)
...a Star of David
...branches that curve
...a dark base

Just Lovely

Use the picture and letter equations to sound out the answer to the question.

Why shouldn't you work by the light of the menorah's candles?

🐝 + **C** + 🐱 − **P** ⬭ THE

🐝 + **U** + ☕ + 🏃 − **A** + **U**

L + OPPOSITE OF LEFT − **R** + **S**

🚗 − **CA** ⬭ THE

ⓞⓕ ⓐ **M** + 👂 + **A** + 💀 − **S**

Delicious Dishes

Many tasty foods are prepared during Hanukkah. Can you fit all of the ones listed into the crisscross? We left some Y-U-M to get you started!

LATKES, BRISKET, CHEESE, SOUR CREAM, FISH, SUFGANIYOT, KUGEL, BABKAS, CHALLAH, APPLESAUCE

Extra Fun:
Latkes (potato pancakes) and sufganiyot (jelly donuts) remind us of the Hanukkah miracle. To learn why, find the letter marked with the dot. Read around the border!

Make Your Own Latkes

Latkes are probably the most popular Hanukkah food. They take a bit of time to make but are well worth it because they are so delicious. Plan at least two hours—it always takes longer than you think, and you can't rush the frying! This recipe makes about thirty latkes.

Important: Be sure to have an adult help you!

What you will need:
6 medium potatoes, peeled and grated (about 6 cups)
1 medium onion
2 eggs
6 tablespoons flour
2 teaspoons baking powder
Salt and pepper to taste
Olive oil or peanut oil for frying

Note: The more starchy the potato, the crisper the latke. But all kinds of potatoes will taste delicious!

What you do:

1. Peel and grate the potatoes.

2. Squeeze extra moisture from the grated potatoes.

3. Mince the onion very fine.

4. Mix potatoes and onions with eggs, flour, baking powder, salt, and pepper in a large bowl.

5. Heat ⅛-inch oil in a heavy skillet on medium heat until a small drop of water sizzles. Don't let it smoke!

6. Use a soup spoon to place scoops of the potato mixture into the hot oil. Don't crowd the pan—fry only about four latkes at a time.

7. Flatten each latke slightly with a spatula as it cooks. Flip the latke when the first side is crispy and brown, about 5 minutes.

It is nice to have two frying pans going at once to speed things up!

8. Put fried latkes on a cookie sheet lined with several layers of paper towels. Place in a warm oven (250°) to drain the excess oil and keep the latkes warm while you fry the rest. Make layers of paper towels and latkes until you are done.

HELPFUL HINTS:

Grating the Potatoes: You can use a box grater to prepare both the potatoes and the onions. We found it easier to use the grating blade of a food processor for the potatoes and the cutting blade to mince the onions very fine.

Squeezing Out the Moisture: You must thoroughly squeeze the extra moisture out of the grated potatoes; otherwise, the batter will be too wet. You can place the grated potatoes in paper towels or cheesecloth to press the juice out. A fun way to de-juice the grated potatoes is to spin them in a salad spinner! Line the basket with cheesecloth, or put the grated potatoes in a mesh colander that fits inside the basket.

Odd Color: As the potatoes are exposed to the air, the batter turns a bit gray. Don't worry! The latkes will taste fine, and the color will disappear as they fry.

Hot Oil: You may need to adjust the cooking temperature under your frying pan several times. The latkes need to sizzle and turn brown on the first side in about 5 minutes, but the oil should not be so hot that it smokes.

Terrific Toppers

Crack the Picture-and-Letter code to sound out two foods that taste great with latkes!

Tabitha's Trick

Tabitha wrote the Hanukkah grocery list. Mom didn't notice until she got to the store that Tabitha had scrambled all the words! Can you write out the list correctly so that Mom can get on with the shopping?

Thanks!

Hee, hee! Mom will love this list!

Well, at least she left me some clues!

PRODUCE:

MEATS:

DAIRY:

FOR BAKING:

RUBTTE
yellow sticks

EKHCICN
cluck cluck

HSFI
scales and fins

SHCEEE
hard milk

LIMK
moo juice

SGEG
brown or white

FEBE
moo meat

STEPTAOO
grate for latkes

NINOO
makes you cry

UGSAR
sweet stuff

ELJLY
donut stuffing

IOL
lamp lighter

RLOFU
not the kind from the florist

Knock on Wood

Collect words with the same number from the grid and write them in their numbered kitchen cabinet. Rearrange the words to get the answer to each knock-knock joke.

1	3	2	1	3	1
Oil	is	dinner!	us	holiday!	love

2	1	4	3	4	3
Doughnut	of	Lettuce	Honey	miracles!	favorite

4	2	2	3
the	eat	anything	-kah

3	1	4	2
my	latkes!	celebrate	before

Knock Knock
Who's there?
Oil.
Oil Who?

1

Knock Knock
Who's there?
Doughnut
Doughnut who?

2

Knock Knock
Who's there?
Honey.
Honey who?

3

Knock Knock
Who's there?
Lettuce.
Lettuce who?

4

So Many Sufganiyot

Sufganiyot are fried, jelly-filled dough-nuts that are sprinkled with powdered sugar. They are traditionally served during Hanukkah, especially in Israel. Can you find some five-letter words hiding in the word SUFGANIYOT? We've provided you with five empty doughnuts to fill, and the first letter of each word.

  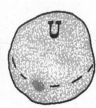

F A S U G

Yummy Doughnuts

There were twenty sufganiyot, but now none are left! Figure out how many doughnuts each of these six friends ate.

1. Sarah took two doughnuts.
2. Noah took one more doughnut than Leah.
3. Leah and Ruth ate the same number of doughnuts.
4. Isaac took three times as many doughnuts as Sarah.
5. Adam took two fewer doughnuts than Noah.

Noah	Isaac	Leah	Sarah	Ruth	Adam

Legend of Judith

Fit the pairs of rhyming words into their proper sentences to learn how Judith's cleverness helped defeat the Assyrian army.

day/away

bed/head

fine/wine

please/cheese

brave/save

1. Judith was _____ to try to _____ her city of Bethulia.

2. "_____ have some _____," she said to Holofernes, the army commander.

3. "It is _____ to drink more _____ ," Judith added.

4. While Holofernes lay drunk in his _____, she cut off his _____!

5. The very next _____, the army went _____!

Cheese Plate

Cheese and dairy products are often eaten during Hanukkah to remember Judith and her bravery. Can you find the eight cheeses hidden on the platter?

```
  A C O T T A G E
 M O G O U S W I S S C M
U O M O Z Z A R E L L A S E
E Z M U E N S T E R E O W N
 Z O D U O G O B R I E I
  R A D D E H C A T T
```

SWISS, CHEDDAR, GOUDA, BRIE, MUENSTER, CREAM, MOZZARELLA, COTTAGE

Challah Twist

Challah is a sweet bread that is often in the shape of a braid. It is served on the Sabbath and many Jewish holidays. Munch your way through this tasty loaf!

START

END

Silly Sentences

What letter can finish all the words in each of these silly sentences about Hanukkah food? Try saying them each three times fast!

__ enjamin __ought __aby __lueberry __abkas.

__dam __te __wfully __ppealing __pplesauce.

__arah __ang __everal __ufganiyot __ongs.

__ucy __oved __icking __ovely __atkes.

__amuel __lurped __avory __uccotash __oup.

Confusing Cookies

The baked butter cookies on the cooling rack all come from one of the rolled-out batches of dough. Which one?

Try this tongue twister: "Betty Botter bought a bit of bitter butter."

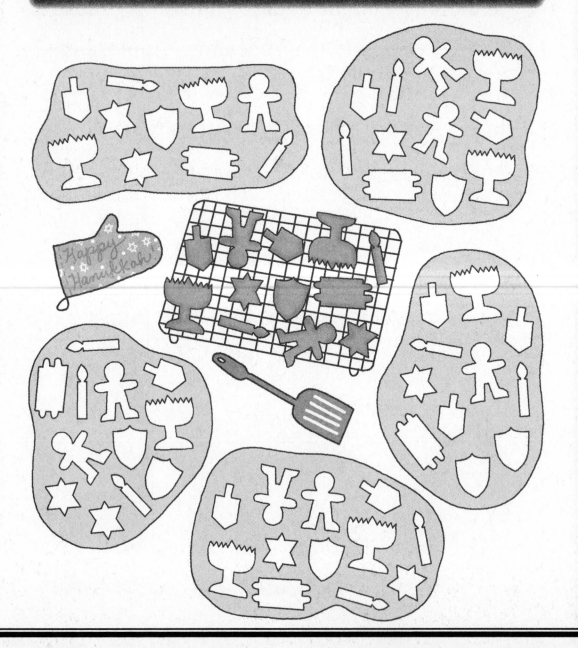

Look carefully at how these bagels overlap. Sometimes the left-hand bagel is on top, and sometimes the right-hand bagel is. Copy down, in order, only the letters in pairs where the right-hand bagel is on top. The letters will spell out a funny joke and its answer.

Helpful Hint: Don't take letters from a pair of bagels with a bite missing!

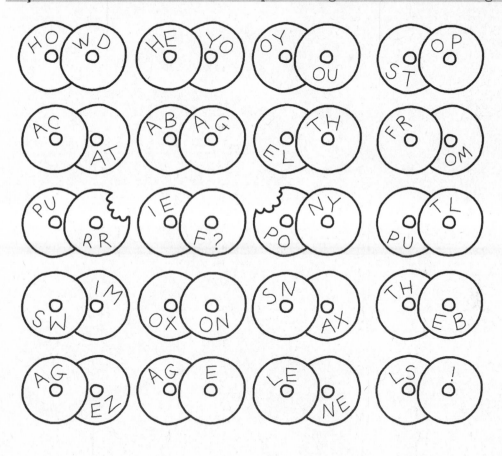

_ _ _   _ _ _   _ _ _ _   _ _ _ _

_   _ _ _ _ _   _ _ _ _   _ _ _ _

_ _ _   _ _ _   _ _ _ _   _ _ _ _ _ !

Kayla's Kugels

A kugel is a baked casserole. It can be served as a side dish at a meal or as a dessert. It all depends what ingredients are cooked into it!

The letters inside these kugels can be read around in one direction or the other. Unfortunately, Kayla has taken a taste from each kugel and one letter is missing! See if you can figure out the different types of kugels her family will be having for Hanukkah this year.

KAYLA!

HMM ~ I HAVEN'T TRIED THIS ONE YET....

1. TTOCESE GECHE

2. INIH UCCC

5. OTA OTA

3. AN O CH

4. RRA O C

Separate

In a kosher home, meat and dairy are not eaten together. Break the Secret Sign code to figure out the foods listed here. The dots in the coded message show the position of the letters. Then write the number of the food on the table where it should be served. Finally, read the Fun Fact and cross out the two foods that should never be eaten!

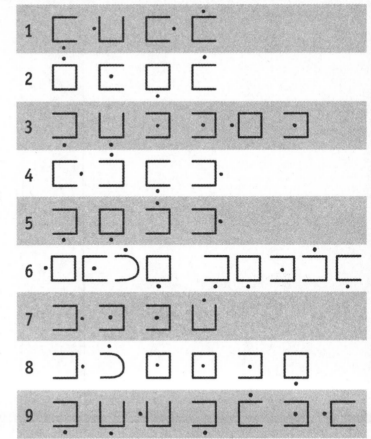

It's a Fact: Traditional Judaism has strict laws about what foods can be eaten and how they must be prepared. Pork and shellfish are strictly forbidden!

MEAT

DAIRY

Hanukkah Havoc

These kids are helping to prepare for Hanukkah—sort of! Can you find at least twenty places where something is not quite right?

One or Eight?

Some children receive a small gift each night of Hanukkah. Others get one larger gift on the last night. In this group, which children get a gift every night? To figure it out, see if the number on their T-shirt is divisible by eight. If it is, they receive nightly presents!

Hidden Gifts

Fill in the boxes that hold the eight G-I-F-T words. They can read up and down, side-to-side, backward, or diagonally. They can even overlap!

F	I	G	T	T	G	I	G	I	F	I	G	I
G	I	I	T	I	I	T	I	T	F	I	G	G
I	G	F	F	I	F	G	I	G	G	I	I	F
F	I	F	F	G	I	F	T	I	I	F	F	G
G	G	T	G	I	G	I	F	G	T	I	T	I
G	F	T	G	I	F	G	I	I	G	G	I	F
T	T	F	I	G	G	I	G	F	G	I	F	I
T	I	G	F	T	I	G	T	F	I	F	F	G
I	I	F	T	I	T	T	G	I	F	I	G	T

Handmade Gifts

Use the letter sets to fill in the blanks and see what Hanukkah gifts the Rosenberg family is making for each other!

Mr. Rosenberg is carving

— — — — ◯ — — — — .

Mrs. Rosenberg is baking

— — ◯ — — — .

Grandma is knitting

— — — ◯ — — .

Sarah is folding

— — ◯ — — — .

Eli is writing

— — ◯ — — .

Phoebe is framing

— — — — — — — — — — ◯ .

Extra Fun: On the last night of Hanukkah, Mr. Rosenberg gives everyone in the family a ticket. Where are they going? Read the circled letters from top to bottom to find out!

Roses are red...

CO IG ES PHS GL

AMI AN OV OK

ALS IES OR TO EMS

IM PHO GRA PO

Beautiful Boxes

These packages are all beautifully wrapped. But which one is for Benjamin? Find the one that has . . .

...straight edges
...dark polka dots
...five ribbon curls

Money, Money

A traditional gift at Hanukkah is money, but it is often called by a different name. Solve the word fractions and write the answers, in order, on the dotted lines. You will learn the common Yiddish name for a gift of Hanukkah cash!

Last ⅓ of HUG
First ¼ of ELEVATOR
Middle ⅕ of CATCH

answer → _ _ _

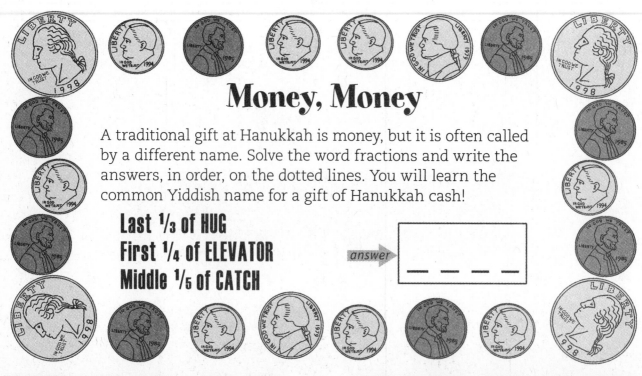

Bags o' Chocolate

These Hanukkah goodie bags are filled with chocolate gelt. If each candy coin was a real coin, which bag would have the most value?

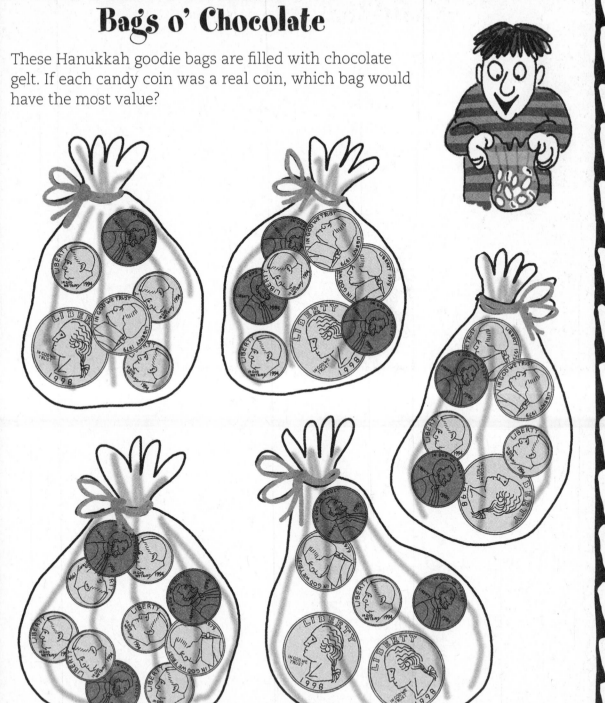

Helping Others

The Hebrew word "tzedakah" means "righteousness," as in "doing the right thing." In the Jewish religion, a person has a duty to do the right thing and give to others in need. Throughout the year, many Jewish families collect coins in a special box to give to worthwhile causes. This is a special duty during Hanukkah too! Color in all the shapes that have the letters C-O-I-N-S to learn a common name for the charity box.

New Boots

Felix got new snow boots as one of his Hanukkah gifts. Can you turn the word GIFTS into the word BOOTS by changing one letter at a time? We left you some hints. One rule: Each time you change a letter, the word you make must be a real word!

GIFTS

_____

_____
(raises up)

_____
(open upstairs rooms)

_____
(what a pirate does)

BOOTS

Shadow Dancer

Candace received a beautiful figurine of a ballerina on the last night of Hanukkah. Which of the shadow music boxes exactly matches the picture?

Jumbled

The Klein children are always given a jigsaw puzzle at the start of Hanukkah. Each night, the family works on it together! Check out the picture from the cover of the puzzle box. Can you spy where each of these pieces will fit?

Hint: The pieces may be sideways or upside down.

Squiggle Giggles

Each of these gift bags contains a child's present.
Use the lines in each bag to draw a fun toy!

For the Needy

Daniel has filled this bag with some of his still-good clothes. He will give them to a local emergency housing shelter. Use a marker to highlight the twelve clothing items listed. When you have finished, use a different colored marker to connect all the Xs. One of Daniel's favorite things to wear will appear!

COAT　　　　　　　　　　**GLOVES**
JEANS　　　　　　　　　　**PANTS**
SHIRT　　　　　　　　　　**SHOES**
SOCKS　　　　　　　　　**SWEATER**
BOOTS　　　　　　　　**HAT**
　　　　　　　　　　　　　　SCARF
　　　　　　　　　　　　　　JACKET

```
            S   T D
      J A H T D
      I A C A T G U O P
    L O S J A W E F P G H K E O
  E A B H A S T C T D P A N S J A K C T E
  I E B G P O Q R E S T U Y Z W O U O R S T F
  L A O H S W E K A T S E V O L G V S O K C S
  I S O J I N C O A T N X X X X X H G F O W P
  K N S K L A S M O X X H P Z I O X X H D E A
  E H T A J N I O X S T T A J E S A B X C P T
  M Y T I A M B X E F A O N S S O C K S X Q N
  Y S R E V W X G S H I R T K L M N A O A X S
  C O J A L L X O O D M E S W E A T E R T X N
  A C M E T O X S W E A T R T H E A I D F X T
  T X X X X X X X X X X X X X X X X X X X C
    O P F A T R H T E Y I I R W I L L V O T O
      Y R B L E E K V I G           N U I
```

Baffling Bills

Esther's aunt gave her two bills for Hanukkah. The total was $25. If one of the bills was not a $5 bill, what denomination bills were given?

Write the amounts in the center of each bill.

Thank you, Aunt Maxine!

You're welcome, bubeleh!

No Boxes

Some families do not give any gifts during the eight days of Hanukkah! Break the Vowel Switch code to find out why.

THUY FUUL THOT THU BUOITAFIL LAGHT EF THU MUNEROH AS GAFT UNEIGH!

"Thumbs Up!" Magnets

Are you looking for a fun Hanukkah gift idea? This is an easy, creative way for you to make great handmade gifts for your family and friends.

What you need:

small plastic frames with magnet
    attached *(one for each person
    on your gift list)*
pencil
several sheets of plain white paper
scissors
stamp pads in different colors
black permanent marker, thin tip

What you do:

- Take the paper insert from inside the plastic frame. Trace it onto the plain white paper. This is the size that your finished thumbprint pictures will be.

- Cut out the rectangle that you have traced and make sure it fits back in the frame. Trim if necessary.

- Cut out a blank insert for each frame you have. Set these aside.

- Take another sheet of white paper for a practice sheet. Press your thumb onto the stamp pad, then firmly onto the paper. Press down hard, then pick straight up. Try not to smear the thumbprint.

- Add details to the thumbprint with the black marker. Try out all kinds of characters to see which ones you like best. Create animals, people, or any other pictures. Use the ones shown here, or make up new ones of your own!

- Try to think of pictures that will please the people on your gift list.

For example, if Aunt Trudy is a cat lover, she would probably like a kitty print!

- Thoroughly wash and dry your thumb before you change colored ink pads.

- When you feel ready to make the gift pictures, create your characters on the small rectangles of paper that you cut out earlier.

- Sign and date your pictures before slipping them into their frames.

- Important: Wash your hands when you are finished. The ink pads may stain your fingers!

Simple Gifts

Gifts don't need to be big or expensive to be enjoyed and appreciated!
How many of these small Hanukkah gifts can you figure out?

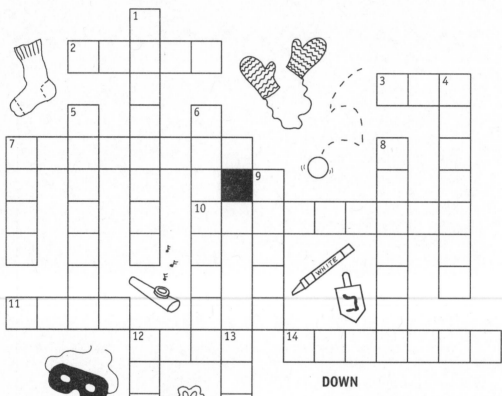

ACROSS

2. 52 come in a deck
3. Sweet, chewy sticks
7. Hair decoration that clips
10. Milk or dark candy gelt
11. Bouncy sphere
12. Covers the face
14. Shrill noisemaker

DOWN

1. Wrist jewelry
4. Hand warmers with thumbs
5. Hanukkah top
6. Small peel-and-put pictures
7. Story holder
8. Waxy coloring sticks
9. Keep your feet warm
12. Watched with popcorn
13. Humming instrument

All Around Town

The Goldsteins want to visit lots of friends this Hanukkah. Create a route that allows them to stop at all nine houses but never travel the same road twice. The Goldsteins have also decided to travel in a particular order: white house, dark house, striped house.

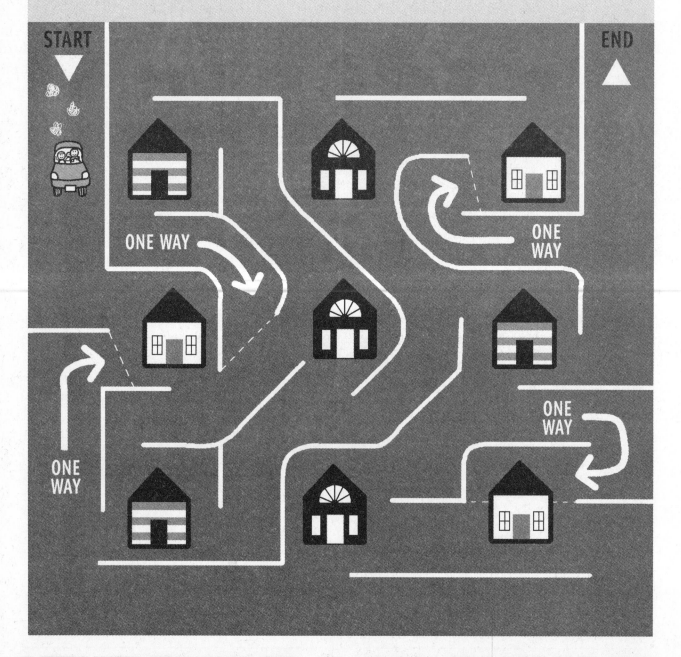

Mezuzah

Like the menorah shining in the window, a mezuzah also identifies a Jewish home. Eleven words are scattered around this page. Put them in the correct blanks to learn more about this special blessing!

RIGHT   PARCHMENT   JEWISH   CASE

TOUCH

The mezuzah is a _____ piece of _____ in a decorative _____ . Written on the parchment are two _____ from the Holy Torah.

WOOD

A mezuzah case can be made of many materials such as _____, _____, metal, or ceramic.

BLESSED

In a _____ home, the mezuzah is hung on the _____ side of the doorway. Jews _____ the mezuzah on the way into and out of the house to remind them that _____ is always there.

GOD

A mezuzah lets everyone know that a Jewish home is _____ .

PASSAGES   SMALL   GLASS

Great Greeting

Many Jews say hello and goodbye to each other using a special word. In Hebrew, this word means "peace." What a perfect greeting to use during the peaceful Hanukkah holy days! Fill in all the shapes containing the letters P-E-A-C-E to learn this wonderful word.

Menorah Materials

If you visited several different Jewish friends, you would probably find that each had a different kind of menorah. Some are fancy, while others are quite simple. Eleven different materials used to make menorahs are listed here. Can you fit them all into their proper place in the crisscross? We've left you a C-A-N-D-L-E to help you out.

BRASS, CLAY, GLASS, GOLD, SILVER, BRONZE, STONE, TIN, WOOD, COPPER, PEWTER

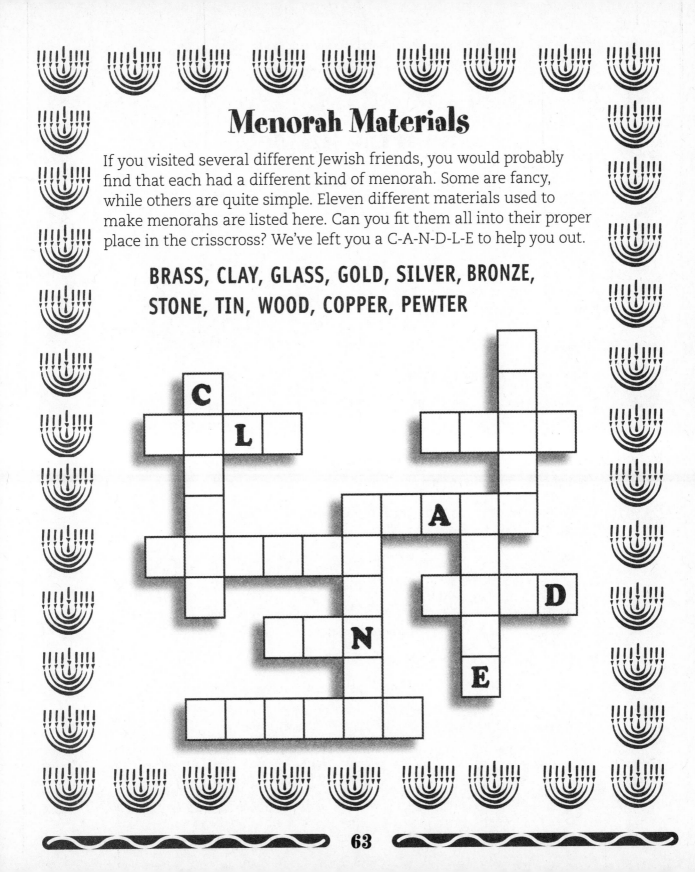

Spin the Dreidel

Playing with the dreidel is a great way
to celebrate Hanukkah with all the
friends you visit!

What you will need:
1 dreidel and a few dozen tokens,
such as candies, chocolate gelt,
pennies, buttons, etc.

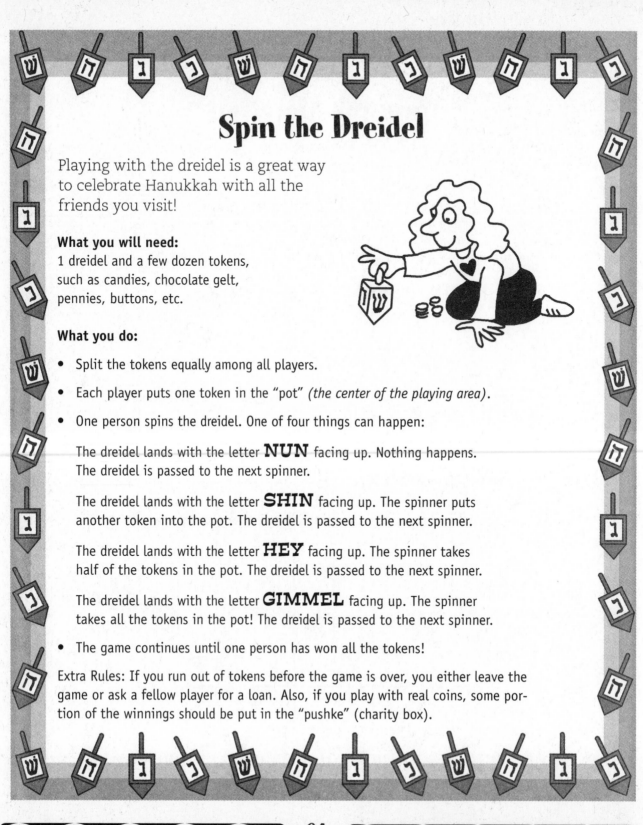

What you do:

• Split the tokens equally among all players.

• Each player puts one token in the "pot" *(the center of the playing area)*.

• One person spins the dreidel. One of four things can happen:

The dreidel lands with the letter **NUN** facing up. Nothing happens.
The dreidel is passed to the next spinner.

The dreidel lands with the letter **SHIN** facing up. The spinner puts
another token into the pot. The dreidel is passed to the next spinner.

The dreidel lands with the letter **HEY** facing up. The spinner takes
half of the tokens in the pot. The dreidel is passed to the next spinner.

The dreidel lands with the letter **GIMMEL** facing up. The spinner
takes all the tokens in the pot! The dreidel is passed to the next spinner.

• The game continues until one person has won all the tokens!

Extra Rules: If you run out of tokens before the game is over, you either leave the
game or ask a fellow player for a loan. Also, if you play with real coins, some portion of the winnings should be put in the "pushke" (charity box).

Use this handy guide to figure out what the player does after he or she spins the dreidel!

TAKE ALL — GIMMEL

DO NOTHING — NUN

TAKE HALF — HEY

PUT ONE IN — SHIN

You Bet

When playing dreidel, you can use a variety of different things as your tokens. Find five possible playing pieces hidden in this dreidel.

BUTTONS
CANDY
NUTS
PENNIES
RAISINS

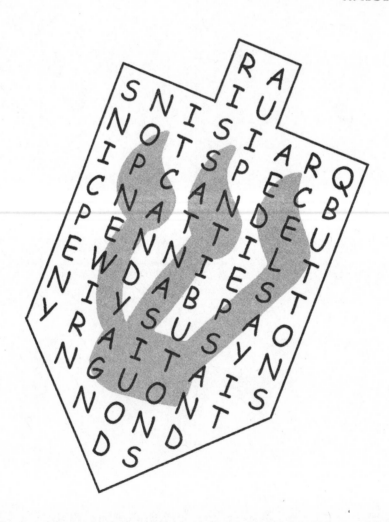

Special Symbols

What do the Hebrew letters on a dreidel stand for? Answer as many clues as you can. Transfer the letters into the numbered boxes. Work back and forth until the answer is revealed!

1A		2G	3D	4F	5D	6G	
7B	8G	9E	10B	11F	12A	13E	
14C	15F	16A	17A	18C	19G	20A	21E
22D	23G	24E	25B	26D			

!

A. Crunchy, red fruit = $\underline{\hphantom{x}}$ $\underline{\hphantom{x}}$ $\underline{\hphantom{x}}$ $\underline{\hphantom{x}}$ $\underline{\hphantom{x}}$
   $\quad\quad\quad\quad\quad\quad\quad\quad$ 1 17 16 12 20

B. A male goat = $\underline{\hphantom{x}}$ $\underline{\hphantom{x}}$ $\underline{\hphantom{x}}$
   $\quad\quad\quad\quad\quad\quad$ 25 10 7

C. Opposite of she = $\underline{\hphantom{x}}$ $\underline{\hphantom{x}}$
   $\quad\quad\quad\quad\quad\quad\quad$ 14 18

D. To rip or shred = $\underline{\hphantom{x}}$ $\underline{\hphantom{x}}$ $\underline{\hphantom{x}}$ $\underline{\hphantom{x}}$
   $\quad\quad\quad\quad\quad\quad\quad$ 22 26 5 3

E. Bambi is one = $\underline{\hphantom{x}}$ $\underline{\hphantom{x}}$ $\underline{\hphantom{x}}$ $\underline{\hphantom{x}}$
   $\quad\quad\quad\quad\quad\quad$ 21 24 13 9

F. Highest playing card = $\underline{\hphantom{x}}$ $\underline{\hphantom{x}}$ $\underline{\hphantom{x}}$
   $\quad\quad\quad\quad\quad\quad\quad\quad$ 15 11 4

G. Opposite of day = $\underline{\hphantom{x}}$ $\underline{\hphantom{x}}$ $\underline{\hphantom{x}}$ $\underline{\hphantom{x}}$ $\underline{\hphantom{x}}$
   $\quad\quad\quad\quad\quad\quad\quad$ 19 8 2 23 6

Hanukkah Checkers

Grab a friend and a standard checkers game to play this Hanukkah version. It is a battle between the Maccabees and the Syrians!

Make a photocopy of the next page. Cut out the twenty-four circles and use rolled tape to attach them to the top of the regular checkers. Tape the Maccabees to one color checker and the Syrians to the other.

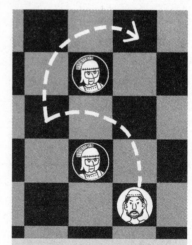

This Maccabee soldier makes a double jump, and captures two Roman soldiers. They are removed from the game.

Rules of the Game:

- Decide who will be the Maccabees and who will be the Syrians (change sides after each game). Each player sets up their "soldiers" on the twelve dark squares closest to them.

- The Maccabees move first and then the armies alternate turns.

- Moves are only allowed on the dark squares, so all moves are diagonal. Soldiers can only move forward one space at a time to an empty square.

- To make a capture, a soldier jumps over the opponent and lands on the empty square diagonally behind him. The captured piece is removed from the board. One soldier can make multiple jumps and captures in a single turn as long as there is a vacant square behind each piece jumped over.

- A soldier must jump if there is a capture to be made.

- If a piece makes it all the way across the board and reaches the last row, it becomes a king. The king gets stacked with a second checker. Make sure the face of your army is on top. Kings move one space at a time, but they can move forward <u>and</u> backward!

- One side wins the game when it has captured all of its opponent's soldiers or have blocked any remaining ones so that they cannot move.

I Spy

Elijah took pictures of the friends he visited one night during Hanukkah. Unfortunately, his camera was stuck on zoom and only small pieces of each friend appeared in the final photos! Can you match each photo to the correct friend?

Sad Rabbi, Glad Rabbi

The rabbi is sad when he realizes how many friends he hasn't had a chance to see this Hanukkah. Cheer him up by making a path through the maze, ending with the glad rabbi in the bottom right-hand corner. Alternate from sad to glad by moving up and down, or side to side, but not diagonally. If you hit a sleepy rabbi, you are going in the wrong direction!

START

END

Golden Gelt

Who will find the most tasty chocolate coins? Follow each path from start to end, and count the gelt you find along the way. Color these coins yellow or gold.

Hey kids, you can only move through the white spaces!

No jumping on the furniture!

Eve

Lisa

Ruth

END   END   END

Hanukkah Hide-and-Seek

Try this version of hide-and-seek with your friends. The tricky part is you have to do the counting in Hebrew!

- Decide which friend is going to be IT. That person covers his eyes and counts very slowly to ten. He should take a deep breath before he begins to count, and another one in between each number to give everyone time to hide.

- Everyone else looks for a good place to hide. Good hiding places include under a bed, in a closet, behind the shower curtain, and so on. Important: Don't hide anywhere you might get locked in or where you have trouble getting enough air!

- When IT has finished counting, he calls out, "Ready or not, here I come!" and the searching begins. The last person to be found is the winner!

- Helpful Hint: Use the word list and pronunciation guide on this page to practice saying the Hebrew numbers before you start to play. Copy the words onto a big piece of paper so you can read them when it is your turn to be IT!

Achat...
Shtayim...
Shalosh...

Counting in Hebrew:

1 = **ACHAT**
(ah-CHAT)

2 = **SHTAYIM**
(SHTA-yim)

3 = **SHALOSH**
(sha-LOHSH)

4 = **ARBA**
(AHR-bah)

5 = **CHAMESH**
(chah-MESH)

6 = **SHESH**
(shesh)

7 = **SHEVAH**
(SHE-vah)

8 = **SHMONEH**
(SHMOH-neh)

9 = **TAY-SHAH**
(TEY-sha)

10 = **ESER**
(EH-sehr)

When Is Hanukkah?

You want to plan a Hanukkah party, but when is Hanukkah? Check out the calendar in your kitchen. You might see that Hanukkah starts in December, or you might find it starting in November! That's because the start of Hanukkah is figured using the Hebrew calendar. This calendar is very different from the one we use daily. Use the decoder to find out why! Write your answer in white pencil.

Fun Fact:
Hanukkah begins at sunset the day before the date on the calendar. This is because a Jewish day begins and ends at sunset, not at midnight!

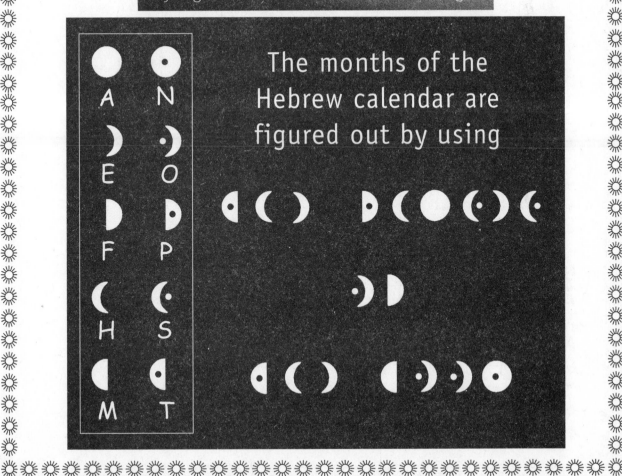

The months of the Hebrew calendar are figured out by using

HEBREW

```
H A N P T P A V
S Y A H E A N U
H E S H V A N R
E K I K E K A A
V T N I T Y O Y
A O U S I V A N
T A N L D T O I
A A L E L O F R
Y D M V O U E H
R A F M A L M S
I R L Y U S H I
A L O L M Z A T
```

GREGORIAN

```
N R J U L Y E S
O C T O B E R E
V M D E L M B P
E E E R I T H T
M A C T R F H E
B T E M P E A M
E S M N A B U B
R U B K J R K E
A G E H S U C R
M U R T A A N H
J A N U A R Y E
R T Y S A Y T S
```

Different Calendars

You are familiar with the months of January, February, March, and so on. These are the months of the Gregorian calendar. The Hebrew calendar also has twelve months but uses completely different names! Hanukkah always begins on the twenty-fifth day of the month of Kislev.

See if you can find the Hebrew and Gregorian months in these two word searches.

Hebrew Calendar Months

TISHRI *(Sept-Oct)*	NISAN *(Mar-Apr)*
HESHVAN *(Oct-Nov)*	IYAR *(Apr-May)*
KISLEV *(Nov-Dec)*	SIVAN *(May-June)*
TEVET *(Dec-Jan)*	TAMMUZ *(June-July)*
SHEVAT *(Jan-Feb)*	AV *(July-Aug)*
ADAR *(Feb-Mar)*	ELUL *(Aug-Sept)*

Gregorian Calendar Months

JANUARY	JULY
FEBRUARY	AUGUST
MARCH	SEPTEMBER
APRIL	OCTOBER
MAY	NOVEMBER
JUNE	DECEMBER

Party Planning

You need a well-organized to-do list when planning a party! Group together all the words that have the same number. Form a sentence with these words and write it on the correct line. You will end up with a list of things to do to get ready for your Hanukkah party.

1. _____

2. _____

3. _____

4. _____

5. _____

6. _____

4 FAVORS	6 THE	5 HOUSE	3 SUPPLIES	1 YOUR	5 THE
2 INVITES	3 A	4 GET	2 GUESTS	3 MAKE	2 YOUR
6 DECORATE	1 ON	5 WHOLE	1 DATE	5 VERY	4 AND
4 GROCERIES	2 AND	5 WELL	2 CHOOSE	5 CLEAN	6 AND
3 SHOPPING	1 A	6 PARTY	3 LIST	1 SET	4 PARTY
1 CALENDAR	6 SET	4 THE	2 SEND	6 TABLE	3 FOR

Interesting Invitations

Miriam is using her computer to send out e-vites, but her fingers aren't on the right keys. Can you figure out her mistake and read her invitation?

E3Q4 R483HEW,

*O3QW3 D9J3 59 J6 YQH7IIQY *Q456.

85 2800 G3 Q5 J6 Y97W3 9H 5Y74WEQ6,

E3D3JG34 W8S5Y, R49J 5Y433 59 38TY5 *J.

23 2800 YQF3 O95W 9R R7H!

O9F3, J848QJ

Perfect Postage

These Hanukkah stamps for the party invitations all look pretty much the same. However, only two of them are exactly alike. Can you find them?

Ernie's Envelopes

When Ernie printed his party envelopes, something odd happened! Look at the list of all the kids in Ernie's class. Can you figure out who will get invitations? Circle their names.

Aaron Singer	Nathan Dreyfuss
Benjamin Mazar	Eve Reiss
Dinah Grossman	Phoebe Bamburger
Rufus Feder	Mara Altman
Cyrus Cohen	Naomi Frankel
Kel Shulman	Zia Kramer
Gideon Bruck	Saul Levy

Where's the Party?

Abby, Leah, Ben, and Daniel all live in the same neighborhood. One of them is throwing a Hanukkah party. Use the clues to decide in which house each child lives. Draw a balloon at the house hosting the party!

CLUES

* Abby lives on West Street.

* Daniel lives diagonally across the street from Ben.

* Leah lives down the street from Abby but on the opposite side.

* Ben lives across the street from Abby

* Leah and Daniel live in the same block but not on the same street.

* Ben does not live on West Street.

* Abby must cross West Street to visit Ben or Daniel.

* The party is at the house on West Street but not on the corner.

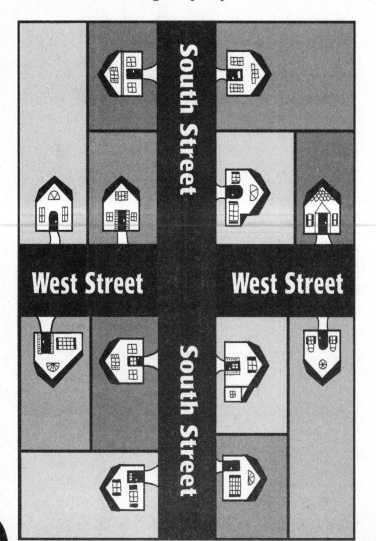

Let's Decorate

Daria is putting up lots of Hanukkah streamers. Can you find the four places where these patterns appear?

Tiptop Word Search

Bernice and her friends are trying to win a new dreidel, or spinning top. They are racing to see who can finish this puzzle first! The tricky part is they have to find fifteen Hanukkah words, but they also have to find twelve words that contain the letters T-O-P.

Hanukkah words

BLESSING, CANDLE, DREIDEL, FIGHT, FREEDOM, JEWISH, KISLEV, LATKE, LIGHT, MACCABEES, MENORAH, MIRACLE, OIL, SONGS, STORIES

Extra Fun:
Each T-O-P shows up as a small picture of a dreidel instead of the letters!

T-O-P words

TOPIC, UNS**TOP**PED, OC**TOP**US, **TOP**AZ, **TOP**PLE, LAP**TOP**, ROOF**TOP**, TREE**TOP**, DESK**TOP**, S**TOP**LIGHT, AU**TOP**SY, S**TOP**WATCH

Helpful Hint:
Use one color marker to highlight all of the Hanukkah words and another color to highlight the T-O-P words.

```
M A C C A B D R E I D E L M E N O R
N E I R P J R T Y T H E Q S O N G S
O P   P L E M C K R C E D   B X O J
W M E D T W I V E I R T H W O S L O
K R B H A I R O   K M I R A C L E B
I W G O U S C Y O L I G H T X H A T
S I W N   H L B N T H I M C L R O O
F W D O S S   L I G H T E H C E E M
M E N O Y H N E C M E R N N L I O K
L S E I R O T S O A T E O T D D O U
  A Z O L E O S H C O E R F E N   N
I N T A R C L I T A H   A E A K N S
S T H K T I S N F B H M R O S I R
Z M E G E F U G O E E F H E H S A P
L E A L L O   U K Y A D D K A L H E
E N U Z L E C A N D L E I N K E I D
S O O   R E O I R E A L L Y I V S I
E R P I L D T H R O O F   E T O L R
N A U G A M N O R R R A H L L I D O
L H R A M A C C A B E E S S O W L O
```

Hink Pinks

The answer to these Hink Pinks are pairs of rhyming words that have the same number of syllables. The last Hink Pink is extra special—it has three rhyming words as the answer! We left you the first and last letter of each word as a holiday hint.

Liquid cooking fat you can depend on =

L _ _ _ L O _ L

A Christmas carol at a Hanukkah party =

W _ _ _ G S _ _ G

Holds waxy light sticks =

H _ _ _ _ S C _ _ _ _ S

Asking for a dairy food politely =

"C _ _ _ _ E, P _ _ _ _ E!"

Playing dreidel over and over =

S _ _ E G _ _ E

The nicest person at the party =

B _ _ T G _ _ _ T

A glowing menorah after dark =

B _ _ _ T N _ _ T L _ _ T

Hanukkah Play

To help remember the miracle of the oil and the fight of the Maccabees against the Syrians, the children put on a special play. At the end of their performance, they spelled out a word with special meaning to the celebration of Hanukkah. Follow the directions to see this important word.

1. **Fill in all the blocks on the left side of each child's sign.**

2. **Fill in all the top blocks for all signs except 5 & 7.**

3. **Fill in all the blocks on the right side of signs 6 & 7.**

4. **Fill in the center block only on signs 2 & 7.**

5. **Fill in all the bottom blocks for signs 3, 4, & 6.**

6. **Fill in the middle three blocks on the right side of sign 5.**

1   2   3   4   5   6   7

Sweet Treats

Solve the picture and letter equations to find some delicious party desserts!

1.

(chef) + E E E E E E

2.

(cheese with mouse) + (cake)

3.

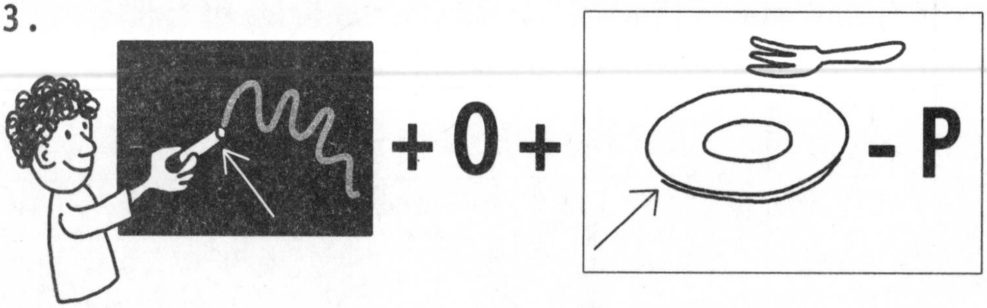

(drawing) + O + (plate) − P

4.

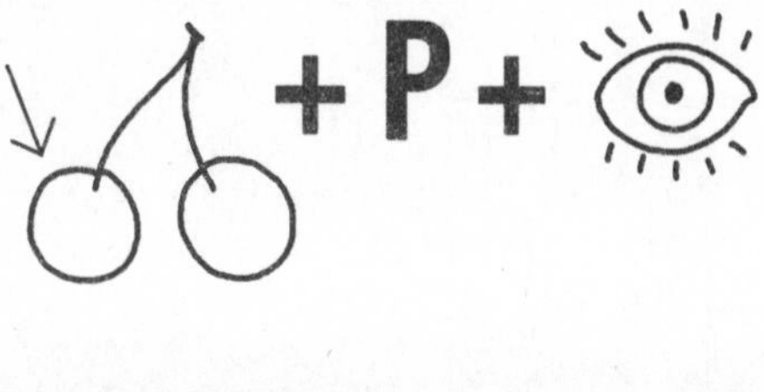

(cherries) + P + (eye)

5.

(deer) + (peanuts)

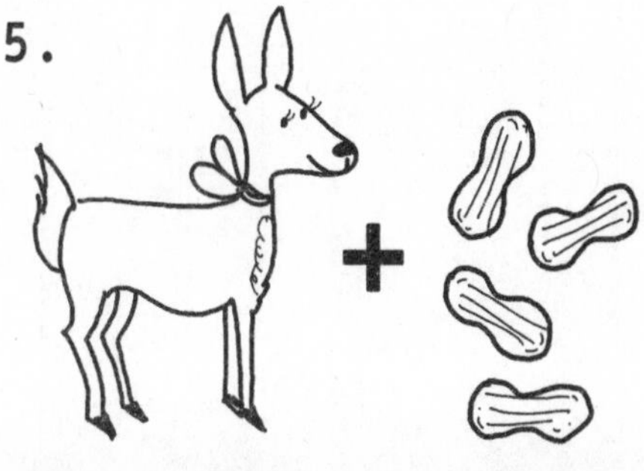

Goodie Bag

Each child at Max's Hanukkah party got to take a goodie bag home. To discover what was inside, use a dark marker or crayon to shade in the numbered boxes that are listed for each row. Remember, rows go across!

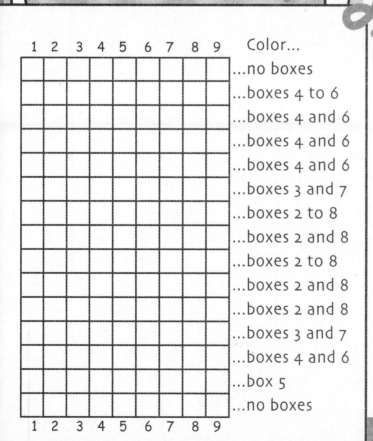

	1	2	3	4	5	6	7	8	9	Color...
										...no boxes
										...boxes 4 to 6
										...boxes 4 and 6
										...boxes 4 and 6
										...boxes 4 and 6
										...boxes 3 and 7
										...boxes 2 to 8
										...boxes 2 and 8
										...boxes 2 to 8
										...boxes 2 and 8
										...boxes 2 and 8
										...boxes 3 and 7
										...boxes 4 and 6
										...box 5
										...no boxes

1 2 3 4 5 6 7 8 9

Fun Fact: The gift in this bag is very small. But a group of enthusiastic students in Montreal, Canada, once built one of these over twenty-two feet tall!

Chapter 7

Hanukkah Crafts

Make a Special Card

You will need a calligraphy marker, or other marker with an angled tip, and a piece of thin white paper. Place the paper over the word. Practice forming the letters, using the shadow of the letters through the paper as a guide. Be sure to write from RIGHT to LEFT. Use your new skill to make a beautiful Hanukkah card!

Fold a piece of heavy paper in half. Write "Hanukkah," just as you have practiced.

Write from RIGHT to LEFT!

Glue on candles cut from blue paper, and add flames of glitter or foil.

Cut a piece of blue paper with decorative scissors.

Glue it inside the card.

With love, YONAH

Write your message here!

חֲנוּכָּה

89

Copy Card

Try this Hanukkah jigsaw card—copy each square into the proper place in the grid to see the design!

Fun Fact: Cut the front of any card into nine pieces to make your own jigsaw!

Yummy!

Jack and Grandpa are making a cupcake menorah. Number these pictures from one to six in the correct order they should happen to accomplish this activity.

Jack's Joke

Figure out this silly joke by crossing out all the letters that appear more than two times. Read the leftover letters from left to right and top to bottom.

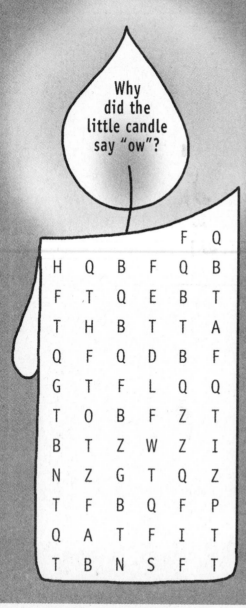

Why did the little candle say "ow"?

				F	Q
H	Q	B	F	Q	B
F	T	Q	E	B	T
T	H	B	T	T	A
Q	F	Q	D	B	F
G	T	F	L	Q	Q
T	O	B	F	Z	T
B	T	Z	W	Z	I
N	Z	G	T	Q	Z
T	F	B	Q	F	P
Q	A	T	F	I	T
T	B	N	S	F	T

Dip, Dip, Dip

Mia and her mother like to make Hanukkah candles by dipping long cotton wicks over and over into hot wax. Each time they dip, the candles get one layer thicker.

Each of the words below start with the letters C-A-N. As you move downward, the words get one letter longer each time! Can you figure out all the words?

A walking stick =
CAN_

Sweet stuff =
CAN_ _

A deep valley =
CAN_ _ _

Water container =
CAN_ _ _ _

People eater =
CAN_ _ _ _ _

Person seeking office =
CAN_ _ _ _ _ _

A melon =
CAN_ _ _ _ _ _ _

Classic Chorus

Use the decoder to discover the chorus to a popular Hanukkah song!

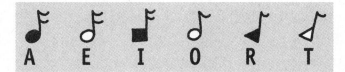

A   E   I   O   R   T

♩H D♩♪♫♪D♪L, D♩♪♫♪D♪L, D♩♪♫♪D♪L,
♪ M♪D♪ ♫♪ ♪U♪ ♪F CL♪Y.
♪ND WH♪N ♫♪'S D♪Y ♪ND ♪♪♪DY,
♪H♪N D♪♪♫♪D♪L ♫ SH♪LL PL♪Y !

Check out the TorahTots Web site to hear the tune to this song:
www.torahtots.com/holidays/chanuka/crafts/dreidelsong.htm

Play a Ka-dreidel!

Make your own kazoo and use it to play the dreidel song!

What you need:
a small cardboard tube
waxed paper
scissors
elastic band
markers or crayons

What you do:
1. Decorate the tube with markers or crayons.
2. Cut a circle of waxed paper, about 5 inches across.
3. Place the waxed paper over one end of the tube and secure it with an elastic band.
4. To play your kazoo, gently hum into the open end of the kazoo.

Quilt Quiz

Anna and Lily have sewn a beautiful Hanukkah quilt. Can you find these three sets of quilt squares?

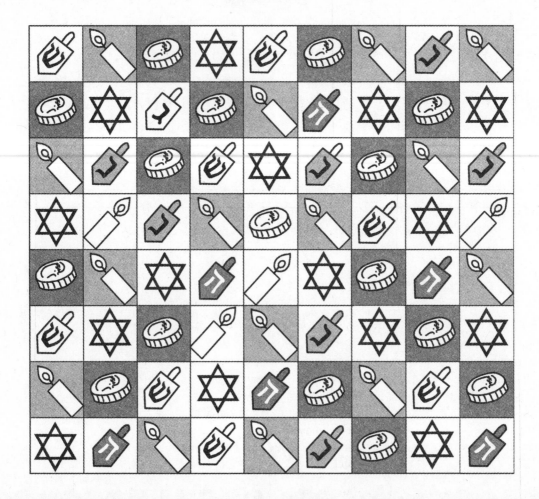

Good Enough to Eat!

Tanya and her friends are making edible dreidels. Looking at the picture, can you answer these questions?

— **Are there more marshmallows or pretzel sticks?**

— **Which Hebrew letter is shown the most times?**

— **How many dreidels can be made?**

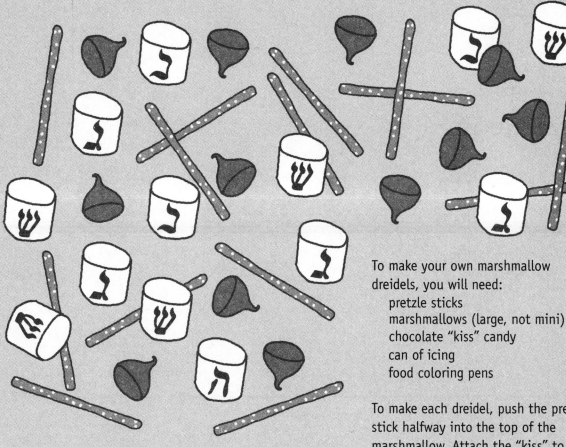

ב ג ה ש
NUN GIMMEL HEY SHIN

To make your own marshmallow dreidels, you will need:
    pretzle sticks
    marshmallows (large, not mini)
    chocolate "kiss" candy
    can of icing
    food coloring pens

To make each dreidel, push the pretzel stick halfway into the top of the marshmallow. Attach the "kiss" to the bottom of the marshmallow with a smear of icing. Write the letters NUN, GIMMEL, HEY, and SHIN on each side of the marshmallow. These dreidels don't spin well, but they taste very good!

Stick to the Stars

Follow these directions to make an easy Star of David ornament to reflect the joy of this Hanukkah season.

What you will need:

newspaper
tacky glue
6 wooden craft sticks
acrylic paint
paintbrush
glitter
clear fishing line

Look, Grandpa!

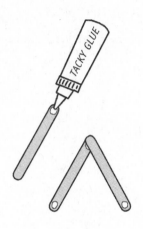

What you do:

- Cover your work surface with newspaper.

- Squeeze a large dot of glue onto the end of one craft stick and lay a second stick on top to form a V. Squeeze two large dots of glue on the ends of the V and lay the third stick across them to form a triangle.

- Make a second triangle in the same way with the other three sticks. Let the glue on both triangles dry completely.

- Lay one triangle on top of the other to form the six-pointed Star of David. Use a pencil to mark where the triangles overlap. Put a large dot of glue at each of these places, press one triangle down on top of the other, and let the glue dry completely.

- Paint the star using acrylic paint. You can add glitter while the paint is still wet.

- Hang the star with fishing line!

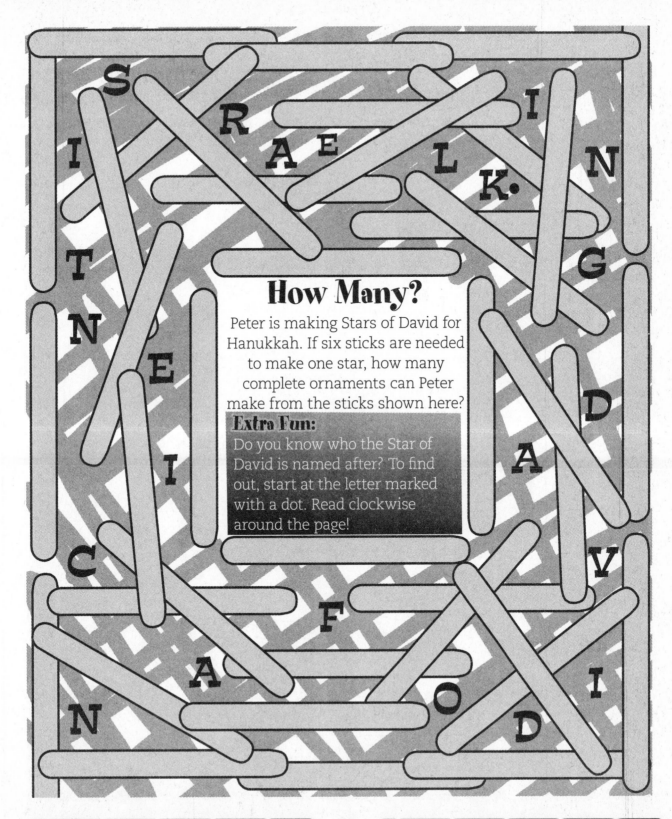

How Many?

Peter is making Stars of David for Hanukkah. If six sticks are needed to make one star, how many complete ornaments can Peter make from the sticks shown here?

Extra Fun:

Do you know who the Star of David is named after? To find out, start at the letter marked with a dot. Read clockwise around the page!

Cookie Cans

Each of these fancy gift cans has a different kind of cookie packed inside. Unscramble the letters to discover each type.

Fun Fact: Use an empty one-pound coffee can and your imagination to make some beautiful cans to fill with your own cookies! Here are some suggestions.

Cover lid with a circle of fabric. Tie with a ribbon or yarn.

Cover can with fancy wrapping paper.

Use a potato or rubber stamp on plain paper.

AMTOAEL　　　**OOACMARN**　　　**SSOMLAES**

Cover the can with plain fabric. Make candles from strips of ribbon. Cut flames from shiny paper, or use glittery pom-poms.

Print or copy a photo large enough to wrap around the can. Wrap clear packing tape smoothly over the photo and all the way around the can.

ATCOCHOLE PHCI　　　**TUEPAN REUBTT**

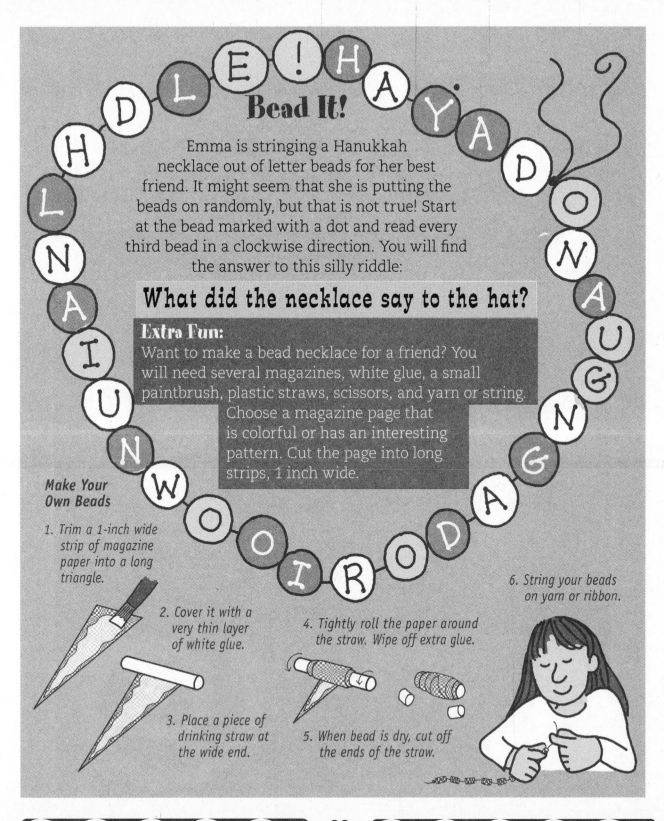

Bead It!

Emma is stringing a Hanukkah necklace out of letter beads for her best friend. It might seem that she is putting the beads on randomly, but that is not true! Start at the bead marked with a dot and read every third bead in a clockwise direction. You will find the answer to this silly riddle:

What did the necklace say to the hat?

Extra Fun:
Want to make a bead necklace for a friend? You will need several magazines, white glue, a small paintbrush, plastic straws, scissors, and yarn or string. Choose a magazine page that is colorful or has an interesting pattern. Cut the page into long strips, 1 inch wide.

Make Your Own Beads

1. Trim a 1-inch wide strip of magazine paper into a long triangle.

2. Cover it with a very thin layer of white glue.

3. Place a piece of drinking straw at the wide end.

4. Tightly roll the paper around the straw. Wipe off extra glue.

5. When bead is dry, cut off the ends of the straw.

6. String your beads on yarn or ribbon.

Chapter 8

Family Celebration

Relax a Little

There is a lot to do to get a house ready for the celebration of Hanukkah. Once the menorah is lit, there is a custom in some families—the ladies get to take a break from all their work! In these households there is only one kind of work that Mom or Auntie can do while the candles are burning. What is it? To find out, fill in the blanks with the names of some common chores, then read the shaded boxes from top to bottom.

Suck up dirt from the floor = V _ _ _ _ U _

Clean the floor with water = _ _ _ P

Match pairs of footwear = S _ _ _ T _ _ _ _ CK _

Fill a suitcase for a trip = _ A _ _

Put away clutter = _ _ _ _ Y _

Wash and dry clothes = D _ _ _ _ _ U _ R _

Get rid of trash = _ _ _ K _ O _ _ _ _ B G _

Which House?

Which home is hosting the family dinner on the last night of Hanukkah? Cross out the kinds of words listed; then read the words that remain on the path to each door.

When you find the correct house, add the numbers along its path to find out what time the party starts!

Cross out words that...
- **have DD in them**
- **start with GR**
- **rhyme with ONE**
- **end with P**

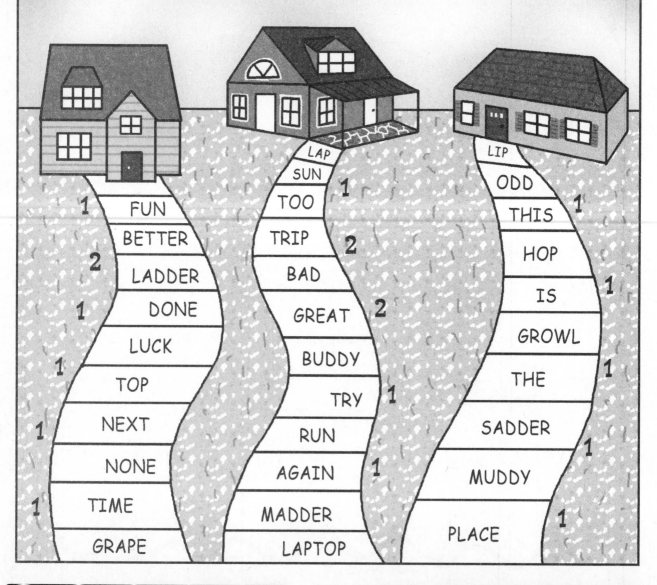

Path 1	Path 2	Path 3
1 FUN	LAP	LIP
BETTER	SUN	1 ODD
2 LADDER	1 TOO	THIS
1 DONE	TRIP	HOP
LUCK	2 BAD	1 IS
1 TOP	GREAT	GROWL
NEXT	2 BUDDY	THE
1 NONE	TRY 1	1 SADDER
1 TIME	RUN	MUDDY
GRAPE	AGAIN 1	1 PLACE
	MADDER	
	LAPTOP	

Fitting Family

Fit all of these relatives into the crisscross.

mother
father
sister
brother
grandmother
grandfather
aunt
uncle
cousin
niece
nephew

Sisters Twisters

How quickly can you figure out these family tongue twisters? An extra letter crowds each twister—take it out to find the answer!

GFRGEDG'SGFGAGMILGYGFRIGEDGGFIFGTYGFAGTGFGISGH.

HAIRRIYIHIATIEDIHAIPIPIYIHANUIKIKIAHIHUIGISI.

BMBAMBA'SBMBENBORBAHBMABDBEBMANBYBMEBMORIBEBSB.

SDISDTEDRDSDALDLYDSDIDTSDSIDNGDINDGSILDLYDSDONDGS.

"Maoz Tzur"

This traditional song, known as "Rock of Ages," is often sung in English and/or Hebrew after the Hanukkah candles are lit. It reminds everyone of the courage of the Maccabees. Break the Number Substitution code (1=A, 2=B, 3=C, and so on) so you can read the lyrics.

18-15-3-11 15-6 1-7-5-19 12-5-20 15-21-18 19-15-14-7

16-18-1-9-19-5 20-8-25 19-1-22-9-14-7 16-15-23-5-18;

20-8-15-21, 1-13-9-4-19-20 20-8-5 18-1-7-9-14-7 6-15-5-19,

23-1-19-20 15-21-18 19-8-5-12-20-5-18-9-14-7 20-15-23-5-18.

6-21-18-9-15-21-19 20-8-5-25 1-19-19-1-9-12-5-4 21-19,

2-21-20 20-8-9-14-5 1-18-13-19 1-22-1-9-12-5-4 21-19,

1-14-4 20-8-25 23-15-18-4 2-18-15-11-5 20-8-5-9-18

19-23-15-18-4 23-8-5-14 15-21-18 19-20-18-5-14-7-20-8

6-1-9-12-5-4 21-19.

Hanukkah Hugs

Find the eleven times the word HUGS shows up in this festive family gathering. See if you can also find four dreidels, two menorahs, and seven Stars of David.

"Oh, Hanukkah!"

The whole family is ready to sing "Oh, Hanukkah," their favorite seasonal song. Unfortunately, the lyrics on the song sheet are missing all of their vowels! Fill in the blanks with the letters A, E, I, O, and U to complete the verses.

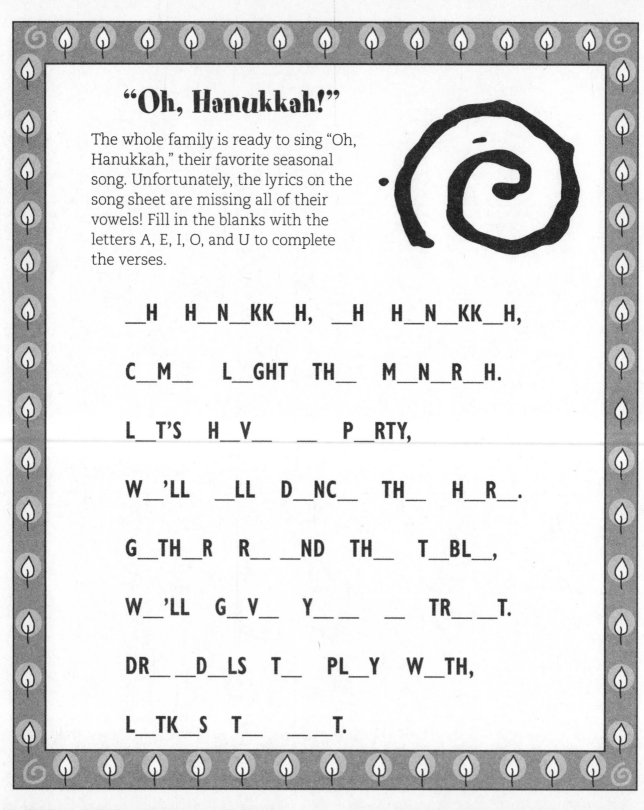

__H H__N__KK__H, __H H__N__KK__H,

C__M__ L__GHT TH__ M__N__R__H.

L__T'S H__V__ __ P__RTY,

W__'LL __LL D__NC__ TH__ H__R__.

G__TH__R R__ __ND TH__ T__BL__,

W__'LL G__V__ Y__ __ __ TR__ __T.

DR__ __D__LS T__ PL__Y W__TH,

L__TK__S T__ __ __T.

Party Lights

START

END

START at the shammas and see if you can light all
the candles before you get to the END!

Around the Table

It is important to remember that the history of Hanukkah is full of sacrifice and acts of courage. During dinner, Uncle Leon tells the story of seven brothers who gave their lives standing up for their religious beliefs. Long ago in Judea, the seven were brought before King Antiochus. Each one was commanded to break the laws of the Torah by worshiping an idol or by eating unclean meat. Each brother refused. As their mother stood by, the king had each of her sons killed.

What was the name of the mother who gave her sons such faith? Each clue suggests a five-letter word ending with E. Write each word into the puzzle. Put the first letter in the outer ring and spell toward the middle. Read the letters in the outer ring.

1. What a cowboy rides

2. Opposite of dead

3. A sound

4. Doctor's assistant

5. Opposite of below

6. Dwelling place with walls and a roof

Quite a Crowd

Help Sophie through the party to her dad.

END

START

How Many?

Check the picture on the Quite a Crowd puzzle. In the blanks below, write how many of each item you see, then find the number and word hidden in the grid.

___ MENORAHS
___ STARS OF DAVID
___ DREIDELS
___ GIFTS
___ RELATIVES
___ CANDLES

```
S T A F M E N O H S T O D
D R E I D E L S N H F O I
B V B V A G I F G W R R V
R A O E V I T I I T I N A
E D X S D S E S S W E E D
L O T M X H M C T O D M F
A R H E O A D A U F Z O O
T A R N B R R N S E I L S
I T E O E O E D F T E G R
V S E V E N I L E O A O A
E I F S T E I E O T U R T
S E N O R M D S M C O R S
```

Double the Fun

At family gatherings, everyone has a hard time telling Todd and Tim apart! Can you find seven differences?

Helpful Hint: It does not count that they are facing in opposite directions.

Happy Ending

Start at letter number one and read the letters in order to find the silly answer to this knock-knock joke!

Knock, knock.

Who's there?

Now eye.

Now eye, who?

4 E	16 H	5 Y	15 T
10 W	20 K	6 E	19 U
22 A	14 U	3 W	11 A
2 O	7 K	17 A	12 B
24 !	23 H	8 N	18 N
1 N	21 K	13 O	9 O

N O W
1 2 3

E Y E
4 5 6

K N O W
7 8 9 10

A B O U T H A N U K K A H !
11 12 13 14 15 16 17 18 19 20 21 22 23 24

Look Again!

Did you think Hanukkah was all over? Not yet! Find each of these picture pieces somewhere in this book. Write the name of the puzzle each piece is from in the space under each box.

Helpful Hint: There is only one piece from each chapter!

1.

2.

3.

4.

5.

6.

7.

8.

Glossary

dreidel

a four-sided spinning top

gelt

money, real or chocolate, traditionally given during Hanukkah

hanukkiah

a special menorah for the candles used during Hanukkah. The hanukkiah holds nine candles—eight candles plus the shammas

Hebrew

the language of the Jewish holy book, the Torah, and the language that is spoken in Israel today

Kislev

the ninth month of the Hebrew calendar. Hanukkah traditionally falls on the twenty-fifth day of this month

latke

a potato pancake fried in oil

Maccabees

a small group of Jews, led by Judah Maccabee, who fought the Syrian army for the freedom to practice their own religion

menorah

a candleholder used for religious purposes that can hold any number of candles

shammas

the servant candle used to light the other candles on the hanukkiah

sufganiyot

jelly-filled doughnuts fried in oil

Yiddish

a combination of German, Hebrew, and other languages of eastern and central Europe

Books

A Hanukkah Treasury

Edited by Eric A. Kimmel (1998)

A timeless collection of stories, recipes, games, crafts, and songs to help you celebrate the joyous Festival of Lights.

A treasury that you will want to refer to year after year.

Celebrate Hanukkah

By Deborah Heiligman (2006)

Fabulous photographs enhance this informative book about how Hanukkah is celebrated around the world.

I Have a Little Dreidel

By Maxie Baum (2006)

A fine picture book version of the classic Hanukkah song. Includes directions for playing the dreidel game and a recipe for latkes.

Hanukkah at Valley Forge

By Stephen Krensky (2006)

A picture book for older children regarding a fictional exchange between George Washington and a young Jewish soldier during the American Revolution. Comparisons are made between the Jews' fight for religious freedom against King Antiochus and America's battle for independence from England. Beautifully illustrated.

Hanukkah Counting Book

By Emily Sper (2001)

This cleverly designed die-cut book guides the reader in counting from one to eight in English, Hebrew, and Yiddish. Along the way, it also presents the familiar symbols and traditions of this holiday.

Websites

→ www.chabad.org/kids

This Web site has a section especially for kids that covers many topics of Judaism, including holidays like Hanukkah. There are games, stories, recipes, arts and crafts, and multimedia activities to enjoy.

→ www.jewfaq.org

Judaism 101 is an award-winning online encyclopedia of Judaism. It covers basic information on Jewish holidays, practices, beliefs, people, places, and much more. It has been growing for ten years and is periodically updated.

→ www.joi.org/dreidel/index.shtml

The Jewish Outreach Institute sponsors this fun site where you can play the dreidel game with a group of animated children. The dreidel music plays in the background throughout the game.

→ www.torahtots.com

A colorful site with a section on Hanukkah devoted to information about the holiday, games and puzzles, coloring pages, virtual greeting cards, songs, and crafts.

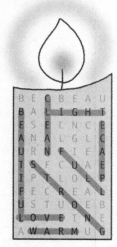

Turn Around • Page vi

Hanukkah Beginnings • Page 2

one before J	between R and T	two after P	first one	four before I	between K and M
I	S	R	A	E	L

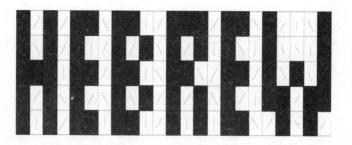

Holy City, Holy Temple • Page 3

The Holy Temple WAS IN THE CITY OF JERUSALEM

Puzzle Solutions

Many Versus One • Page 4

THE JEWS BELIEVE IN ONLY ONE GOD.

What Is B.C.E.? • Page 5

BEFORE COMMON ERA

The Common Era began at year 1. That means if you are in the year 2010, the Common Era began 2010 years ago! Dates that have a B.C.E. after them are even longer ago than that — these dates are <u>before</u> the Common Era started!

Brave Decision • Page 6

WHOEVER IS FOR GOD, FOLLOW ME!

Rebellion! • Page 7

1. BATTLE
2. COMBAT
3. ATTACK
4. RESIST
5. REVOLT

Which Son? • Page 7

JUDAH MACCABEUS

Why Fight? • Page 8

A. Opposite of day

N I G H T
31 35 36 5 14

B. Frozen water

I C E
27 22 33

C. Not rich

P O O R
16 2 15 8

D. Part of your foot

T O E
24 29 10

E. Solid

F I R M
7 21 32 13

F. Follows two

T H R E E
20 25 17 9 23

G. Lion's noise

R O A R
28 12 18 3

H. Opposite of dry

W E T
30 6 4

I. Not hot

C O L D
19 38 34 11

J. Overdue book penalty

F I N E
1 37 39 26

	1J F	2C O	3G R		4H T	5A H	6H E		
	7E F	8C R	9F E	10D E	11I D	12G O	13E M		
14A T	15C O		16C P	17F R	18G A	19I C	20F T	21E I	22B C	23F E
	24D T	25F H	26J E	27B I	28G R		29D O	30H W	31A N
	32E R	33B E	34I L	35A I	36A G	37J I	38I O	39J N	!

Big in Battle • Page 9

ARMORED ELEPHANTS

Tough Guys • Page 10

The Maccabees would strike like a...

Puzzle Solutions

Cleaning House • Page 11

R	E	D	E	D	I	C	A	T	I	O	N

The word "Hanukkah" means "dedication" in Hebrew.

Lighting the Lamp • Page 12

To work very hard = **T OIL**

Circle of lacy paper = **D OIL Y**

To wind rope in a circle = **C OIL**

Go bad, like sour milk = **S P OIL**

Great disorder = **T U R M OIL**

To cook under a flame = **B R OIL**

Dirt in the yard or garden = **S OIL**

Thin sheets of aluminum = **F OIL**

Amazing Events • Page 13

Wonderful things that cannot be explained are called...

M I R A C L E S

Light Up the Night • Page 15

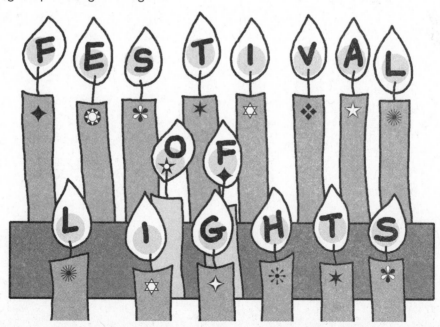

FESTIVAL OF LIGHTS

Cover Up • Page 16

TO SHOW RESPECT FOR GOD

In Those Days • Page 18

G+1 C-2 Q-3 S+2 J+1 L-1 E+4 B-1 K-3

H A N U K K I A H

Shining Servant • Page 21

A wrapped Egyptian = M U M M Y

Moving through water = S W I M M I N G

Curved punctuation mark = C O M M A

Living forever = I M M O R T A L

To shine with faint light = S H I M M E R

A kid's word for stomach = T U M M Y

Day Is Done • Page 17

START

SUN	DAY	BREAK	FAST	RAN
DOWN	RIGHT	LEFT	TOWN	SOME
POUR	HAND	MADE	ME	COME
HOLD	BAG	UP	GRADE	BACK
ON	LADY	SHIP	SCHOOL	YARD
TIME	BUG	LAMP	HOUSE	HOLD

END

Three Blessings • Page 20

Blessing 1 (*recited every night of Hanukkah*)

Blessed are You, Lord our God, Sovereign of the universe, Who has sanctified us with Your commandments, and commanded us to kindle the Hanukkah light.

Blessing 2 (*recited every night of Hanukkah*)

Blessed are You, Lord our God, Sovereign of the universe, Who made miracles for our ancestors, in those days at this time.

Blessing 3 (*recited only on the first night of Hanukkah*)

Blessed are You, Lord our God, Sovereign of the universe, Who has kept us alive, sustained us, and brought us to this season.

Why Use a Shammas? • Page 21

Hanukkah candles represent a miracle.
1   2   3   4   5

They should not be used for anything else!
6   7   8   9   10   11   12   13

Puzzle Solutions

Proper Lighting • Page 24

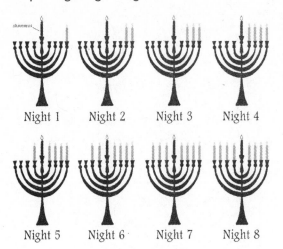

Night 1   Night 2   Night 3   Night 4

Night 5   Night 6   Night 7   Night 8

Time to Share • Page 26

5 minutes
15 minutes
30 minutes
1 hour
12 hours
24 hours

B	E	C	A	U	S	E		N	O		S	I	N	G	L	E
D	A	Y		O	F		H	A	N	U	K	K	A	H		
I	S		M	O	R	E		I	M	P	O	R	T	A	N	T
T	H	A	N		T	H	E		O	T	H	E	R	S	.	

Eight in a Row • Page 26

Show Off • Page 25

IN THE WINDOW

Counting Candles • Page 27

First Night = 2

Second Night = 3

Third Night = 4

Fourth Night = 5

Fifth Night = 6

Sixth Night = 7

Seventh Night = 8

Eighth Night = 9

total number of candles used 44

The Shafner family would use 44 x 4 candles = 176 candles.

Monika's Menorah • Page 28

Just Lovely • Page 29

Because the beautiful lights are the symbols of a miracle.

Delicious Dishes • Page 31

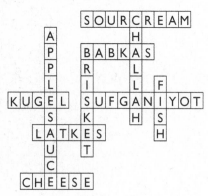

Answer to why latkes and sufganiyot remind us of the Hanukkah miracle:

Because they are both fried in oil!

Tabitha's Trick • Page 34

PRODUCE : *POTATOES, ONION*

MEATS : *BEEF, CHICKEN, FISH*

DAIRY : *MILK, BUTTER, CHEESE*

FOR BAKING : *FLOUR, SUGAR, JELLY, OIL, EGGS*

Terrific Toppers • Page 33

SOUR CREAM

APPLESAUCE

Knock on Wood • Page 35

1. Oil of us love latkes!

2. Doughnut eat anything before dinner!

3. Honey-kah is my favorite holiday!

4. Lettuce celebrate the miracles!

So Many Sufganiyot • Page 36

Some letters can start several words! Here are the ones we found. How about you?

F FANGS FOUNT

A ANTSY AGONY

S STUNG SNOUT SATIN SAINT STAIN

U USING UNITY

G GOATS GIANT GUSTY

Puzzle Solutions

Yummy Doughnuts • Page 36

Legend of Judith • Page 37

1. Judith was BRAVE to try and SAVE her city of Bethulia.
2. " PLEASE have some CHEESE ," she said to Holofernes, the army commander.
3. "It is FINE to drink more WINE ," Judith added.
4. While Holofernes lay drunk in his BED , she cut off his HEAD !
5. The very next DAY , the army went AWAY !

Cheese Plate • Page 38

Challah Twist • Page 38

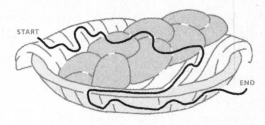

Silly Sentences • Page 39

Benjamin Bought Baby Blueberry Babkas.
Adam Ate Awfully Appealing Applesauce.
Sarah Sang Several Sufganiyot Songs.
Lucy Loved Licking Lovely Latkes.
Samuel Slurped Savory Succotash Soup.

Confusing Cookies • Page 40

Bagel Burglar • Page 41

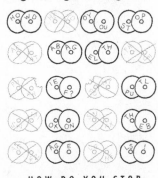

HOW DO YOU STOP
A BAGEL THIEF?
PUT LOX ON THE BAGELS!

Kayla's Kugels • Page 42

1. COTT**A**GE CHEESE
2. **Z**UCCHINI
3. **S**PINACH
4. CARRO**T**
5. **P**OTATO

Separate • Page 43

1 MILK
2 ~~PORK~~
3 CHEESE
4 LAMB
5 ~~CRAB~~
6 SOUR CREAM
7 BEEF
8 BUTTER
9 CHICKEN

MEAT — 4 9 7

DAIRY — 1 6 8 3

Hanukkah Havoc • Page 44

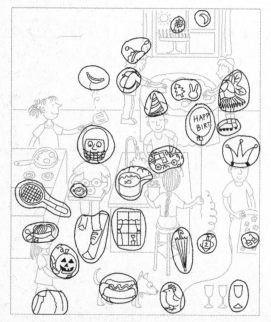

One or Eight? • Page 46

Hidden Gifts • Page 46

F	I	G	T	T	G	I	G	I	F	I	G	I
G	I	I	T	I	I	T	I	T	F	I	G	G
I	G	F	F	I	F	G	I	G	G	I	I	F
F	I	F	F	G	I	F	T	I	I	F	F	G
G	G	T	G	I	G	I	F	G	T	I	T	I
G	F	T	G	I	F	G	I	G	I	G	G	I	F
T	T	F	I	G	G	I	G	F	G	I	F	I
T	I	G	F	T	I	G	T	F	I	F	F	G
I	I	F	T	I	T	T	G	I	F	I	G	T

Handmade Gifts • Page 47

Mr. Rosenberg is carving
A N I M A L S.

Mrs. Rosenberg is baking
C O O K I E S.

Grandma is knitting
G L O V E S.

Sarah is folding
O R I G A M I.

Eli is writing
P O E M S.

Phoebe is framing
P H O T O G R A P H S.

Puzzle Solutions

Beautiful Boxes • Page 48

Bags o' Chocolate • Page 49

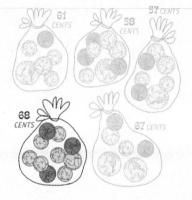

Helping Others • Page 50

Money, Money • Page 48

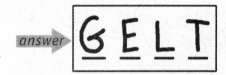

answer

G E L T

Yiddish is a language that combines Hebrew, an old style of German, and Slavic words. It is mostly spoken by Jews who live in Eastern Europe.

New Boots • Page 51

GIFTS

LIFTS
raises up

LOFTS
open upstairs rooms

LOOTS
what a pirate does

BOOTS

Shadow Dancer • Page 51

Jumbled • Page 52

Squiggle Giggles • Page 53

Your drawings will look different than these!

For the Needy • Page 54

No Boxes • Page 55

THEY FEEL THAT THE BEAUTIFUL LIGHT OF THE MENORAH IS GIFT ENOUGH!

Baffling Bills • Page 55

Answer: One bill was not a $5 bill, but the other one <u>was</u>! The second bill was a $20 bill.

Simple Gifts • Page 58

Puzzle Solutions

All Around Town • Page 60

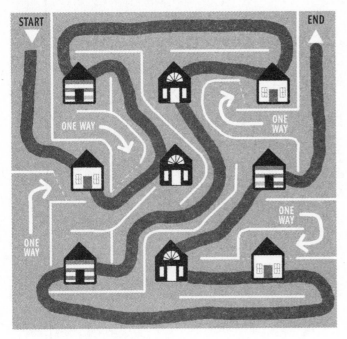

Great Greeting • Page 62

Mezuzah • Page 61

The mezuzah is a <u>SMALL</u> piece of <u>PARCHMENT</u> in a decorative <u>CASE</u>. Written on the parchment are two <u>PASSAGES</u> from the Holy Torah.

A mezuzah case can be made of many materials such as <u>WOOD</u>, <u>GLASS</u>, metal, or ceramic.

In a <u>JEWISH</u> home, the mezuzah is hung on the <u>RIGHT</u> side of the doorway. Jews <u>TOUCH</u> the mezuzah on the way into and out of the house to remind them that <u>GOD</u> is always there.

A mezuzah lets everyone know that a Jewish home is <u>BLESSED</u>.

A mezuzah is usually thin and rectangular in shape, but it does not have to be. Some are simple, others colorful and ornate. The most important thing is the Holy Torah scroll that's inside the mezuzah case, not the case itself.

Menorah Materials • Page 63

You Bet • Page 66

I Spy • Page 70

Sad Rabbi, Glad Rabbi • Page 71

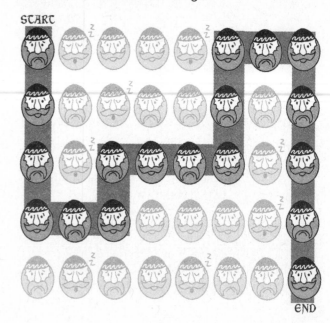

Special Symbols • Page 67

A. Crunchy, red fruit = **A P P L E**
$\overline{1}$ $\overline{17}$ $\overline{16}$ $\overline{12}$ $\overline{20}$

B. A male goat = **R A M**
$\overline{25}$ $\overline{10}$ $\overline{7}$

C. Opposite of she = **H E**
$\overline{14}$ $\overline{18}$

D. To rip or shred = **T E A R**
$\overline{22}$ $\overline{26}$ $\overline{5}$ $\overline{3}$

E. Bambi is one = **D E E R**
$\overline{21}$ $\overline{24}$ $\overline{13}$ $\overline{9}$

F. Highest playing card = **A C E**
$\overline{15}$ $\overline{11}$ $\overline{4}$

G. Opposite of day = **N I G H T**
$\overline{19}$ $\overline{8}$ $\overline{2}$ $\overline{23}$ $\overline{6}$

1A	2G	3D	4F	5D	6G
A	G	R	E	A	T
7B	8G	9E	10B	11F	12A	13E
M	I	R	A	C	L	E
14C	15F	16A	17A	18C	19G	20A	21E
H	A	P	P	E	N	E	D
22D	23G	24E	25B	26D		
T	H	E	R	E	!	

Dreidels in Israel have slightly different letters. They use the Hebrew letter Pay, representing the phrase "A Great Miracle Happened <u>Here</u>." Dreidels outside Israel have the Hebrew letter Hay, representing the phrase "A Great Miracle Happened There."

Puzzle Solutions

Golden Gelt • Page 72

When Is Hanukkah? • Page 75

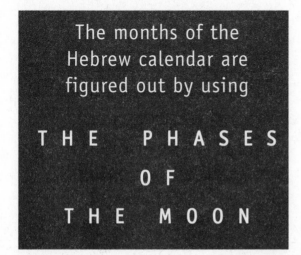

The months of the Hebrew calendar are figured out by using

THE PHASES OF THE MOON

Different Calendars • Page 76

Party Planning • Page 77

1. Set a date on your calendar.

2. Choose your guests and send invites.

3. Make a shopping list for supplies.

4. Get the groceries and party favors.

5. Clean the whole house very well.

6. Decorate and set the party table.

Interesting Invitations • Page 78

To decode the message, choose the letter one row down and one key to the right of each letter that Miriam typed.

. . . .

DEAR FRIENDS,

PLEASE COME TO MY HANUKKAH PARTY.

IT WILL BE AT MY HOUSE ON THURSDAY,

DECEMBER SIXTH, FROM THREE TO EIGHT PM.

WE WILL HAVE LOTS OF FUN!

LOVE, MIRIAM

Perfect Postage • Page 79

Ernie's Envelopes • Page 79

Aaron Singer	Nathan Dreyfuss
Benjamin Mazar	Eve Reiss
Dinah Grossman	**Phoebe Bamburger**
Rufus Feder	Mara Altman
Cyrus Cohen	**Naomi Frankel**
Kel Shulman	Zia Kramer
Gideon Bruck	Saul Levy

Where's the Party? • Page 80

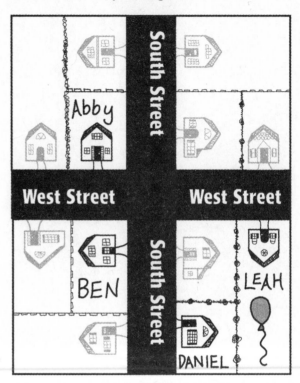

Let's Decorate • Page 81

Puzzle Solutions

Hink Pinks • Page 84

Liquid cooking fat you can depend on =
L O Y A L   O I L

A Christmas carol at a Hanukkah party =
W R O N G   S O N G

Holds waxy light sticks =
H A N D L E S   C A N D L E S

Asking for a dairy food politely =
"C H E E S E ,   P L E A S E !"

Playing dreidel over and over =
S A M E   G A M E

The nicest person at the party =
B E S T   G U E S T

A glowing menorah after dark =
B R I G H T   N I G H T   L I G H T

Hanukkah Play • Page 85

Sweet Treats • Page 86

1. **Cookies**
2. **Cheesecake**
3. **Chocolate**
4. **Cherry Pie**
5. **Donuts**

Goodie Bag • Page 87

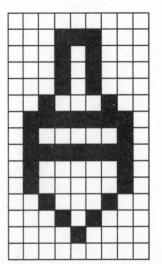

Tiptop Word Search • Page 83

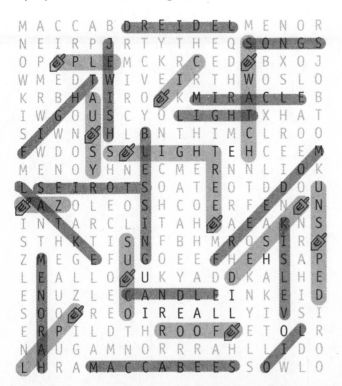

Copy Card • Page 90

	A	B	C
1	HAPPY		
2			
3	HANUKKAH		

Yummy! • Page 91

Jack's Joke • Page 92

Why did the little candle say "ow"?

He had glowing pains!

Classic Chorus • Page 93

OH DREIDEL, DREIDEL, DREIDEL,
I MADE IT OUT OF CLAY.
AND WHEN IT'S DRY AND READY,
THEN DREIDEL I SHALL PLAY

Dip, Dip, Dip • Page 92

A walking stick =
CAN**E**

Sweet stuff =
CAN**D**Y

A deep valley =
CAN**YO**N

Water container =
CAN**TEE**N

People eater =
CANN**IBAL**

Person seeking office =
CAN**D**I**DATE**

A melon =
CAN**TALOUPE**

Quilt Quiz • Page 94

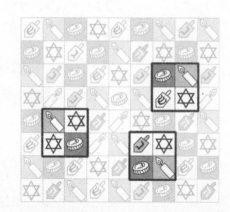

Puzzle Solutions

Bead It! • Page 99

You go on ahead and I will hang around!

How Many? • Page 97

1. Peter can make six complete Star of David ornaments with the sticks shown here. He needs three more sticks to be able to make a seventh ornament.

2. The Star of David is named after King David of ancient Israel.

Cookie Cans • Page 98

 OATMEAL   MACAROON   MOLASSES
CHOCOLATE CHIP   PEANUT BUTTER

Good Enough to Eat! • Page 95

1. There are more pretzel sticks (15) than marshmallows (14).
2. The Hebrew letter Shin appears most.
3. Three dreidels can be made.

Relax a Little • Page 101

V A C U U M

M O P

S O R T   S O C K S

P A C K

T I D Y

D O   L A U N D R Y

T A K E   O U T   G A R B A G E

Which House? • Page 102

Fitting Family • Page 103

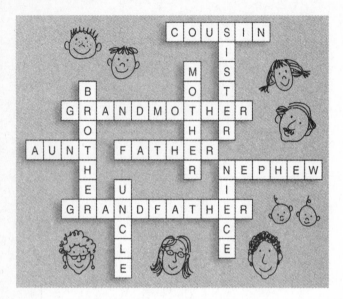

Sisters Twisters • Page 103

Fred's family fried fifty fat fish.

Harry hated happy Hanukkah hugs.

Mama's menorah made many memories.

Sister Sally sits singing silly songs.

"Maoz Tzur" • Page 104

"Rock of Ages, let our song praise thy saving power; Thou, amidst the raging foes, wast our sheltering tower. Furious they assailed us, but thine arms availed us, and thy word broke their sword when our strength failed us."

Fun Facts: The first verse of this song thanks God for the deliverance of the Jewish people from oppressors. The next three stanzas tell the story of liberation and the Exodus from Egypt. The fifth verse tells the story of Hanukkah.

Puzzle Solutions

Hanukkah Hugs • Page 105

Party Lights • Page 107

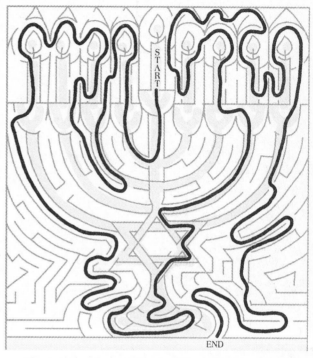

"Oh, Hanukkah!" • Page 106

OH HANUKKAH, OH HANUKKAH,

COME LIGHT THE MENORAH.

LET'S HAVE A PARTY,

WE'LL ALL DANCE THE HORA.

GATHER ROUND THE TABLE,

WE'LL GIVE YOU A TREAT.

DREIDELS TO PLAY WITH,

LATKES TO EAT.

Around the Table • Page 108

The mother's name was Hannah.

Quite a Crowd • Page 109

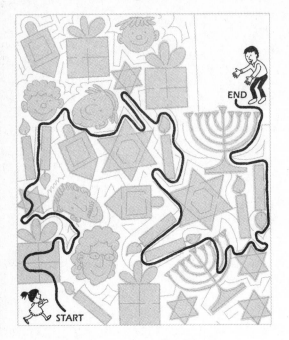

Double the Fun • Page 110

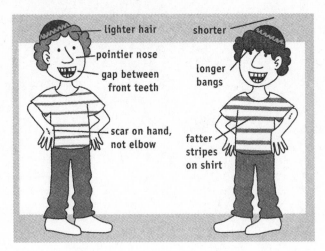

lighter hair

shorter

pointier nose

longer bangs

gap between front teeth

scar on hand, not elbow

fatter stripes on shirt

How Many? • Page 110

2 MENORAHS

7 STARS OF DAVID

3 DREIDELS

4 GIFTS

5 RELATIVES

8 CANDLES

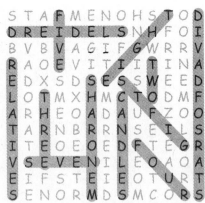

Happy Ending • Page 111

Knock, knock. *Who's there?*

Now eye. *Now eye, who?*

N O W   E Y E
K N O W   A B O U T
H A N U K K A H !

Puzzle Solutions

Look Again! • Page 113

1. Which Son?

2. Monika's Menorah

3. Yummy Doughnuts

4. New Boots

5. Spin the Dreidel

6. Hanukkah Play

7. Stick to the Stars

8. Around the Table